AGENT
OF
PEACE

AGENT OF PEACE

*Emily Hobhouse and her
Courageous Attempt to End
the First World War*

JENNIFER HOBHOUSE BALME

To my Grandchildren
May they have a good life and have the courage to do what is right
for the benefit of humankind

JENNIFER HOBHOUSE BALME is the grand-niece of Emily. She worked in the publicity department of the WRVS for many years. On her father's death she inherited a trunk of Emily's papers, on which this book is based. She is the author of *To Love One's Enemies: The Work and Life of Emily Hobhouse*, published by the Hobhouse Trust. She lives in British Columbia.

Cover illustrations: *Front:* A young Emily Hobhouse; Troops crossing snow-covered ground going to the trenches near Bazentin in France in February 1917. (Mary Evans Picture Library); *Rear:* American women delegates to the first International Congress of Women on board the Peace Ship. (US Library of Congress)

First published 2015

The History Press
The Mill, Brimscombe Port
Stroud, Gloucestershire, GL5 2QG
www.thehistorypress.co.uk

British Library Cataloguing in Publication Data.
A catalogue record for this book is available from the British Library.

ISBN 978 0 7524 6118 9

Typeset in Bembo 11/14pt by The History Press
Printed in Great Britain

CONTENTS

FOREWORD

BY DR BIRGIT SUZANNE SEIBOLD PHD

It is a great honour to write the foreword for Jennifer Hobhouse Balme's book *Agent of Peace*. Jennifer Hobhouse Balme is not only the grand niece of Emily Hobhouse, she is the greatest and the most important of all the Emily Hobhouse researchers and holds the Hobhouse papers. Her first book, *To Love One's Enemies*, is proof of her thorough research.

Emily Hobhouse is probably best known in South Africa because of her enormous involvement with the Boers who had been interned in the concentration camps during the Anglo-Boer War.

British officials found her a nuisance and sent a Ladies' Commission, instead of her, to the concentration camps. The living conditions became slightly better. After the war, Emily Hobhouse carried on to help, and founded spinning, weaving and lace schools for South African women.

When she came back to Britain, there were the first signs of an upcoming war. During the First World War, Emily Hobhouse joined the International Women's League for Peace and Freedom and she worked for more than three months in Amsterdam. She travelled with a German escort from Switzerland to occupied Belgium to investigate the conditions of the Belgian non-combatants. She also reported on the state of destruction of every Belgian town she visited. She was forbidden to speak to the Belgians or to travel into the war zone. From Belgium she travelled to Berlin and met the German Foreign Secretary, Gottlieb von Jagow. She also enquired into the food and health situation in Germany. In Ruhleben, she visited the civilian internees camp and found, unlike in South Africa at the time, no raging sicknesses, no starvation and no deaths. The trouble in the camp was primarily mental – captivity was having a depressing, even maddening effect on many men.

When she returned to England, Emily Hobhouse wanted to lay her information before the British Foreign Secretary, Sir Edward Grey. She had three main objectives: to get peace talks moving, to obtain the release of civilian internees and to get better food and supplies to the Belgians. However, Sir Edward Grey did not want to talk to her. Instead she was questioned by Scotland Yard.

In this book, Jennifer Hobhouse Balme publishes, for the first time, documents of that time. The reader finds most interesting letters relating to the peace movement, journal entries and a short diary by Emily Hobhouse herself.

It is a fascinating book to read.

Birgit Seibold
Ludwigsburg,

Dr Birgit Seibold was born and still lives near Stuttgart, Germany and specialised at Tübingen University on the effects of British colonisation in Africa. She is the author of *Großbritannien und die Kolonialisierung Swazilands* (Great Britain and the Colonialisation of Swaziland) and *Emily Hobhouse and the Reports on the Concentration Camps during the Boer War 1899–1902*. She is currently working on her new project, another book on Africa.

INTRODUCTION

In the preface to *To Love One's Enemies*, I explained that I gleaned most of the information that I used from a trunk of papers I inherited from my father, Emily Hobhouse's nephew. This trunk was the treasure chest that enabled me to expand on official sources to provide an interesting narrative. The book covered Emily Hobhouse's work in the Anglo-Boer War 1899–1902 and also her life in a more general way. The aim, which I believe was accomplished, was to show that Emily Hobhouse did not exaggerate the condition of the camps, which were set up by the British Army for the families of Afrikaner nationals fighting to retain their independence, and that, in trying to improve conditions, she was not a traitor.

Emily Hobhouse was in fact a remarkable and fearless woman. In the middle of the First World War she managed to visit occupied Belgium and Germany. A chance meeting with the German Foreign Secretary, Gottlieb von Jagow, led her to believe that peace talks were possible. She wrote a Journal about her trip but, because of the scope of *To Love One's Enemies* and the length of the Journal, I was unable to include it in that book. There was also extra information, some on small scraps of paper, which had to be studied. It is for this reason I have come up with this book, *Agent of Peace*, and its sequel, *Living the Love*.

Agent of Peace provides the background for Emily Hobhouse's own Journal and describes her efforts to bring about a negotiated peace. Emily Hobhouse was a pacifist with an overriding belief that international disputes should be solved through dialogue. Unlike many of her compatriots, she had seen war at first hand and knew what devastation and misery it could cause. She was an English patriot whose actions went against the times. England, and its ideals, was the great love of her life.

Her efforts have been studied by myself and others. In particular I would like to commend Diane Clements Kaminski who wrote her PhD thesis on Emily Hobhouse, and Birgit Seibold who, although her PhD thesis only covers the Anglo-Boer War, had many ideas on fields for research. Dr Seibold has been especially helpful with her work, and insights, into the German Official Archives – she has also provided help with translations. Without her, this work could not have been produced. I would also like to thank Lord Newton for his help and for introducing me to his grandfather's diary.

Emily Hobhouse lived in the days when the telephone was in its infancy and our modern reliance on technology did not exist. She and her friends were letter writers. It has been the greatest help to be able to find the letters she wrote to her brother, Leonard (L. T.) Hobhouse, and to some especial friends in South Africa and elsewhere. Most notable amongst these were Mrs Isabella Steyn, wife of the former President of the Orange Free State, South Africa, and General Jan Christiaan Smuts who held many important posts in both the South African government and also with the imperial government in London. Letters to Jane Addams in the United States and Dr Aletta Jacobs in the Netherlands are also included.

I would like to express special thanks to my family and also the many people who have helped with typing and vetting the manuscript, especially Sarah Walker. I would also like to thank Giordano Venturi, for help with the Italian translations.

In the letters that are reproduced in this book, I have maintained the abbreviations 'wh' for 'which', 'govt' for 'government', 'cirčes' for 'circumstances' but have written out 'and' for '&' as the latter always seems clumsy.

1

A CORNISH
BACKGROUND

Born in 1860, at a time when women had no status and were expected to be good, obedient and pure, Emily Hobhouse was the youngest of four girls. Her brother, Leonard (L.T. Hobhouse, the noted sociologist and thinker), was four years her junior. Her father, Reginald, was rector of the small Anglican parish in east Cornwall and was later appointed as one of the two archdeacons for the Cornish diocese.

The girls were educated at home and as they grew up, besides sports, art and music, their time was given over to good works, but when their mother died all the fun went out of the house. Their father became reclusive and Emily, as the last remaining girl at home, found the life of a Victorian spinster more and more repressive. Her only outlet was visits to her uncle and aunt, Arthur and Mary Hobhouse. They asked her to be hostess for them when they were in the country. With her quick wit and sweet singing voice she was an asset to any party. Arthur Hobhouse had been in India as the law member of the Governor General's council. He was now a peer of the realm and a member of the Judicial Committee of the Privy Council, the highest court of appeal in the British Empire.

When her father died in 1895, Emily wondered what she could do. Through the wife of Edward Benson (their former bishop in Cornwall who had become Archbishop of Canterbury, the senior bishop in the Anglican

Church), she went to Minnesota to carry out welfare work for the Cornish miners who had emigrated there. She found they were doing well, but there was plenty of work helping other miners – for example, she visited the sick and those in prison, started a library and organised entertainments. She also fell in love and became engaged to be married. With plans for her fiancé to follow her, she went to Mexico to purchase a ranch where they could grow coffee and pineapples. Unfortunately the relationship came to nothing. She returned to London to study child welfare and try her hand at writing.

Emily was always interested in current affairs and *The Times* was delivered daily, even in Cornwall. This she read at meals to her austere father but she had to be careful not to let him know of her Liberal views. He was a staunch Conservative, although Arthur and her brother Leonard were Liberals who believed in the rights of small nations.

In 1899 the Anglo-Boer War broke out. It was really an issue about the gold mines in the Transvaal, South Africa. The Boers (Afrikaner people) had trekked hundreds of miles north of the British Colony at the Cape of Good Hope because they, and the people of the Orange Free State, wanted to be independent of British rule, and the British now wanted their say in the operation of their new territories. Because of his judicial position, Arthur Hobhouse was not able to take part in politics. However, some of his friends, including Leonard Courtney, the independently minded Liberal Unionist MP for the Hobhouses' constituency in Cornwall, formed a South African Conciliation Committee. Emily, who knew Leonard Courtney, entered wholeheartedly into the campaign to find and execute a resolution to the conflict. She spoke publicly, and went on to form a relief fund for the South African women and children who were being herded into camps after their farms had been burnt or destroyed as part of British policy.

Emily went to South Africa to take relief and found the conditions there were very bad. She did what she could there, and then in England, to get them improved. Her actions won for her the ire of the British government but led to the establishment of a Ladies Commission led by Millicent Fawcett[*] to investigate the camps. Emily was not permitted to take part, but their findings showed her to be correct and eventually lasting improvements

---

[*] Millicent Fawcett 1847–1929 was a woman with whom Emily often crossed swords. She was the very competent widow of a blind MP from a neighbouring Cornish constituency and was president of the National Union of Women's Suffrage Societies (NUWSS). Her sister was Elizabeth Garrett Anderson, the first qualified woman doctor in England.

were made. Meanwhile Emily had tried to go to South Africa again to see if she could do something useful, but she was deported.

South Africa became one of her life's passions. She went back soon after the war and prodded the government in the annexed territories (Orange Free State and the Transvaal), especially the Transvaal, to help rebuild the devastated country. She also developed a scheme of Home Industries – spinning, weaving and lace-making – to encourage young women to take pride in their accomplishments. This scheme was later taken over by the home government.

Emily made many friends among the Afrikaner community, including Mrs Isabella (Tibbie) Steyn, the wife of the former President of the Orange Free State, and the brilliant young lawyer Jan Smuts, who had been a general in the Boer Army and was now in government. When in England, Emily introduced him to the British Liberal elite.

Emily returned from South Africa in 1908 a sick woman suffering from neuritis, lumbago and a heart condition which was to incapacitate her for the rest of her life. She was an invalid and could not climb stairs. Cold weather plagued her, though she felt better in the summer warmth. She was not, however, totally inactive. She took part in the suffrage movement and was elected Chair of the People's Suffrage Federation whose members included Leonard Hobhouse, Bertrand Russell and John Galsworthy. The People's Suffrage Federation's programme was 'one man one vote; one woman one vote' so differed from the suffrage proposals of Millicent Fawcett which advocated votes for women over 30 with some property qualifications, and no alteration in the male vote. Men at the time could have multiple votes. Equality, the Federation's dream, did not finally take place until 1946. Emily spent the winters in Rome where she acquired a flat (apartment) and the climate was milder.

In 1913 Emily returned to South Africa to unveil the monument in Bloemfontein to commemorate the 26,000 women and children who had died in British camps. She became sick but her speech was read for her. While she was there 'Mahatma' Gandhi appealed to her – the Indian community in South Africa was suffering and under great pressure. Emily persuaded him to have patience and was able to facilitate a meeting between Gandhi and Prime Minister Botha with whom she was staying, and thus helped resolve the 'Indian' problem. Much later she told a friend that she considered Gandhi to be far and away the greatest man she ever met.[1] When she died in 1926 Gandhi wrote a glowing tribute to her.[2]

2

THE BEGINNING

For working people the August bank holiday, the first weekend of August, was a wonderful time of year. All those who were able took trains to the sea and paddled in the water, ate ice cream or winkles (a local speciality) and crowded the piers to play the slot machines or to listen to the local band. But in 1914 the festive mood was dimmed by the sudden possibility of war with Germany. Young men, however, were excited. Their boring lives could now have new meaning as they could travel to and see places they had only dreamt about. Besides, everyone said a war could not last long. However, more thoughtful people were wary. Leonard Hobhouse wrote to his sister, Emily, on 2 August: 'It is the most serious crisis in our lifetime. We are evidently in the greatest danger.'[1]

Leonard was a member of the Neutrality League. Long fearing that war might break out, he and his group had written to the *Manchester Guardian*, of which he was a director, warning of the possible catastrophe and pointing out that Britain was not obligated to go to war. In fact he had two letters in that paper of 3 August with the same object. Emily had also written pointing out the misery of war to non-combatants.

The crisis had been pending for years. Britain had watched with dismay as Germany built up its armaments and its navy. Many influential Germans, including the historian Treitschke, encouraged the German public with ideas of expansionism as a way to become a great power. This was what many wanted, an aspiration shared by their Kaiser, Wilhelm II, a grandson of Queen Victoria. Wilhelm was both Emperor and Supreme Commander of the Armed Forces so had considerable power. The Chancellor, Theobald von Bethmann Hollweg was appointed by him. In the German parliament, Reichstag, only the nobles could hold office. The system was archaic. There were many in Germany who wanted reform – not war.

The present crisis was triggered at the end of June 1914 by the assassination in Bosnia of Archduke Franz Ferdinand, heir to the throne of Austria–Hungary. The perpetrator was a Serb national. Austria–Hungary responded angrily with a plan to incorporate the vulnerable Balkan country of Serbia into its own territory. It had only recently incorporated Bosnia. They got German support on 23 July. That made things worse. Czarist Russia mobilised to support Serbia and France supported Russia.

The Germans feared they would be fighting on two fronts, against Russia and France, and decided to take action against the French whom they hoped to quickly defeat. The French had made minor incursions into Germany but, because the Franco-German border was heavily fortified, the Germans formulated a plan to attack France through Belgium. Britain had guaranteed Belgian neutrality under a treaty of 1839. Prussia (Germany) and France had been signatories. Chancellor Bethmann Hollweg sarcastically referred to this Treaty as 'a scrap of paper'.

On Friday, 1 August, the German Army violated Luxembourg's neutrality. The Kaiser telegraphed his cousin King George V of Britain stating that he would not attack France, if France offered neutrality guaranteed by the British fleet and Army.[2]

British action was uncertain. The government did not trust the Kaiser. The Cabinet was split. The City – the financial district – was against war. Henry 'H.H.' Asquith, the British Prime Minister, felt that it rested with Germany to keep the peace. He was concerned about the possible government resignations and felt that if Sir Edward Grey, the Foreign Secretary, resigned, he would follow. He believed in a strong France and that the British Navy must retain control of the English Channel.[3]

Emily had been working to get everyone she could to stand against war. The *Manchester Guardian's* editor, C.P. Scott, told her that he was trying to get meetings organised, and the Bishop of Hereford wrote to her that he had written to every incumbent in his diocese asking for action. She urged David Lloyd George, Chancellor of the Exchequer and future Prime Minister, with whom she had campaigned in the Anglo–Boer War: 'to take a bold and noble stand against the very idea of England taking up arms ...' She told him in the outright language she used: 'We Liberals cannot trust Imperialists.' She also wrote to Ramsay MacDonald, another future Prime Minister and to Keir Hardie, the leader of the Independent Labour Party – both of whom stood for peace.[4]

Since the Anglo–Boer War, women who wanted to have the vote and their say in public affairs had become increasingly active in many countries. They had a worldwide organisation, the International Woman Suffrage Alliance (IWSA), with a newspaper, *Jus Suffragii*, published in London and abroad. Many believed in peace. Rosika Schwimmer, a Hungarian described as a fiery feminist, was press secretary and correspondent for various papers. With Millicent Fawcett, vice president of the Alliance, she organised a peace rally in London for the holiday Monday, 4 August. Millicent was criticised for her action. Lord Robert Cecil, a strong supporter of her suffrage programme in Parliament, reminded her that in order to have male support her members must be shown to act 'responsibly'. After this they followed the government line.[5] Millicent regarded Emily as a traitor for her work in the Anglo–Boer War and specifically did not want her there; in this she was gratified.[6]

Emily was unwell and staying in Oxford.

However, hopes for peace were short-lived, for by the time the rally had started German Battalions had begun their march through Belgium. Britain had promptly issued an ultimatum that unless the German Army withdrew by midnight they would be in a state of war. Germany did not withdraw.

On 5 August Leonard wrote to Emily:

> We can only exchange sorrowful feelings today ... My view now is that we can say nothing about neutrality or make no criticism of policy until the country is out of danger ... I wrote Ll[oyd] G[eorge] a strong letter yesterday saying that if he did not leave the Govt the Radical party was ... broken. But war being declared I should not urge him to do so now until the naval question is settled ...[7]

Leonard feared a major naval battle. He was also worried about conscription. His son, Oliver, aged 22, was a scholar at Oxford University.

The war feeling in Britain was so strong that all the principal newspapers, including the *Manchester Guardian*, gave full support to the government. Leonard explained gloomily to Emily, 8 August: 'A paper wh occupied itself with attacks on the war might live for three weeks, but hardly for more.' He continued:

I am not affected by the White Paper wh I have read, as it is clear that Grey, [Sir Edward Grey, British Foreign Secretary] (1) never warned Russia that we shd not back her in the quarrel. Had he done so she wd probably have withdrawn (2) made no attempt to bargain our neutrality against Belgian integrity – a bargain which Germany tentatively approached, and might conceivably have accepted.

Next, as to mediation. You will fret yourself in vain if you talk of it now … If Germany wins she will annex Belgium and dismember France. If we win we shall impose such terms on Germany as will prevent her from being the menace that she has been for Western Europe for 40 years. You must remember that the whole of the armed peace, the doctrine of force wh has taken possession of Europe, and formed it into a camp, is Prussian in origin. Since 1871 [Franco-Prussian War] no Frenchman has had an easy mind. If France wins she will rightly demand the cessation of this menace. It will therefore be useless to talk of mediation until the combatants are exhausted or one is beaten. It is miserable, but it is best to face the facts.

It is bitter for me to realise all this. All our hopes for political and social progress are shattered once and for all … As to Liberalism, it died last Monday. There will, I expect, be a coalition Govt, the Irish will be thrown over, and a small handful of radicals and Labour men will be left. We may write *finis* to our work, and hope that civilization may rise again elsewhere.[8]

So Leonard was for supporting the war while the danger lasted. He believed in the rights of small nations, and the reports of atrocities committed by the Germans as they moved through Belgium must have strengthened his resolve. To Emily war was obscene and nothing could mitigate that. After stating that she always longed to go to Germany she gave her position on the first page of the Journal, which she wrote later. She entitled it:

The Story of My Visit to Germany
June 7 – June 24, 1916
During the Great War

From the very beginning of the War – viz in 1914 I was filled with a longing to go to Germany. Holding as I do, that a War is not only wrong in itself, but a crude mistake I stand wholly outside its passions and feel, while it lasts, a spectator of a scene I deplore, but with which I am in no sense a part. I give, have given and will give nothing to any fund to aid war or warriors. My small means are devoted entirely to help non-combatants who suffer in consequence of war and in supporting every movement making for peace. I believe it useless to soften or civilize war, that there is no such thing as 'Civilized War'; there is war between civilized peoples certainly but as we now see that becomes more barbarous than war between barbarians. I believe the only thing is to strike at the root of the Evil and demolish War itself as the great and impossible Barbarity. Hence all the Governments concerned in making this War are to blame in my eyes, none better than the others though possibly some worse. They follow blindly an outworn and impossible system that must be swept away. I blame them all and am against them all equally. On the other hand my heartfelt sympathies lie with all the peoples of Europe, sacrificed, ruined and destroyed by their blind incompetent rulers. They are also to blame in so far as they allow their better judgment to be led astray by their rulers and do not rise up in a body to stay the tide of bloodshed. But they are to be pitied for the poverty, starvation, misery and universal ruin fall upon their shoulders, besides disease destruction and countless worse evils …[9]

Emily was often unwell. Her doctor from Italy, Dr Francesco Forlani, wrote to her, in flowery Italian on 11 August: 'However good your health situation may be, every preoccupation or apprehension can be extremely dangerous for you. So, be strong and don't listen to the noble voices from your spirit which will incite you.'[10]

For the moment she took his, and Leonard's, advice, but she wrote to her South African friend Jan Smuts, a prominent member of the government there, on 8 August: 'It would be some satisfaction if we could put Grey in a battleship by himself and William II in another and let those two sink each other if they are so anxious to.' She had little sympathy with Grey's policies or the people with whom Britain was allied and she did hope South Africa would be able to stay out of the conflict.[11]

But, the Dominion countries of Australia, New Zealand and Canada had followed Britain into war and the Union of South Africa which also had Dominion status felt obligated to follow suit. Prime Minister Louis Botha thought the Union's role would be a passive one but he was at once called on to capture the ports in German South West Africa, now Namibia, a matter on which he said he would have to consult the Union parliament.

Rosika Schwimmer, active as ever, wrote to Emily on 18 August, saying she was leaving for the United States to see President Wilson and Mr Bryan, the Secretary of State, to put before them a concrete plan for mediation. She wanted a note from Emily expressing her belief in the necessity of urgent mediation. Emily wrote back on 21 August in the style she kept for such occasions saying that she honoured the spirit that prompted Rosika's journey, though quite unaware of her plan, and said:

> It would be a fine lesson for the World if America, like some great mediating Angel, put forth her arm, and stayed the Nations, ere greater carnage comes. Alas! I fear it is both too late and too early for such action on her part. Yet to America many of us look, trusting that She will exercise moral influence, and fulfil that lofty destiny amongst the Nations of the World which we once dreamt was England's high calling. But again the use of physical force has triumphed and now America alone can intervene to uphold higher influences.[12]

Soon Emily herself was spurred into action. She had long been interested in the Quakers, otherwise known as the Religious Society of Friends. The Friends had suffered from religious restrictions in the past, and although by now they had equal freedom, their approach to war was different. Many were pacifists. A Christian Pacifist conference had been convened in Konstance, Germany, on the eve of the war. After leaving the conference Dr Friedrich Siegmund-Schultze, a German Lutheran pastor, and Henry Hodgkin, an English Quaker, took a pledge that, as they were one in Christ, they could never be at war with each other and that they would continue in a life of service. In England this led to the foundation of the Fellowship of Reconciliation.[13] Naturally Emily was interested in this group.

She wrote a flyer addressed to women throughout Europe – a church-going population would have recognised the quotation used to head the appeal:

To Women Throughout Europe
'He took them up in His arms, put His hands upon them and blessed them.'*

Fellow Women,

The war is crushing helpless millions. These are mostly women and children. In Galicia, Serbia, Poland, Belgium, East Prussia, France and elsewhere the people are perishing.

Relief, however colossal, can but touch the fringe of the want.

If the war continues, die they must.

We ask: Must it continue? Can any good come by further blood-shed to weigh against such evil which could not be better attained by agreement and goodwill.

A hundred years ago men proclaimed they fought, as each country asserts it is fighting to-day, 'to secure the rights, the freedom, and the independence of all nations'.

War failed to secure those objects then; can we reasonably suppose it will do so now? ...

[She appealed to England to show the way and continued] Will you not plead on their [the children's] behalf ere it be too late.[14]

Meanwhile, in South Africa, trouble was brewing. Naturally the wounds and sorrows of the Anglo-Boer War had not healed and some people among the Afrikaner community, including the old and revered General de la Rey, felt this was the time to break with England. But on 15 September, on his way home after a special parliamentary session which had approved action, he was accidentally shot.[15]

Unrest followed and on 26 October it was announced that rebellion had broken out. Three Boer generals were involved, the famous De Wet, whom Emily knew, Beyers and Kemp, and there were also other commanders. Their effort was generally thought to be not well coordinated.

---

* Mark, Ch 10 v16.

On 28 October, Leonard was in touch with Emily:

> You will feel with me that, whatever the origins and cause, the outbreak of civil war in S. African Union is an unspeakable calamity. You can influence a good number there who may be wavering and my suggestion is that you send a wire to Mrs Steyn [her friend, the wife of the ex-President of the Orange Free State]: 'Trust South African women will prevent outbreak of civil war.' At the same time the message would be given to the press.

If she agreed, he would have to contact Harcourt, the Colonial Secretary, about it. On 30 October Leonard wrote again: 'On receipt of your evening telegram I sent a note to Harcourt by special messenger and received a reply from him at 11.39 p.m. saying "please send cable but don't use my name."' The words Emily used were 'I appeal to you to urge South African women to prevent civil war.' Leonard told her she had done what she could 'and if you only deter one doubting person from leaving his home and risking his neck in a mad enterprise it will be worth it.' Emily received a cable back reading 'Utmost being done Mrs Steyn' and told Leonard he could use it as he wished.[16]

Emily wrote to Isabella 'Tibbie' Steyn (they were lifelong friends but remained formal in writing):

> C/o Barclay & Co.Ltd.,**
> 137 Brompton Road,
> London S.W.
> Oct 29 /14

Dearest Mrs Steyn

My thoughts are with you and the President in these days of sorrow and tension. This World's War is piercing into every life. I know the form it is taking in South Africa will pierce deeply into yours and with varying emotions.

Today I ventured to cable to you to urge South African Women to stop Civil War with one voice. I thought remembering the Past and its Pain, its Dead and the old oft repeated … 'Never again War in

---

** Emily used her bank address for many letters as she was continually moving around and the bank was prepared to keep the letters for her.

South Africa between Whites' the women might rise in a body headed by your influence and demand that the men on both sides lay down their arms.

The censorship is strict and this may never reach you.

I long for more news and for news I can rely on, but I have little time to write and if the President is ill neither probably have you.

I send this to state the mere fact of having cabled to you to send my love and sympathy to you all.

Yrs ever

Emily Hobhouse

P.S. Of course I could not go to Italy this year, so I am in Cornwall and we look after Belgium refugees. Their tales are the same in every particular I listened to 14 years ago – the war-look stamped on their suffering faces just as those Boer women looked – but their sufferings are less for they are received here with open arms and every kindness is shown to them – and there is no want and sickness amongst them such as we knew of old.[17]

With her mind on South Africa Emily wrote to Jan Smuts:

I cannot bear to think that dear De Wet and Beyers and Kemp will meet a rebel's death. You have asked too much of human nature ... I write in a hurry to implore you if these men are captured ... not to shoot them unless in open fight. The issue might be awful – an internecine struggle – an enmity never forgiven. They are brave, good men. Keep them in prison till the end but do not execute them, do not, do not, do not.[18]

As Leonard was still for supporting the war. Emily wrote to him on 3 November 1914: 'However I suppose you are now friends again with the Government, and having fallen on the neck of Lloyd George you could maybe get him to intervene about the S African rebels if there is any idea of the extreme penalty wh I fear.'[19]

In time De Wet and Kemp were captured, while Beyers drowned trying to cross a swollen river. Only Jopie Fourie, a sharpshooter commander, was court-martialled and shot, an issue Smuts was not allowed to forget.[20]

At Christmas Emily wrote a letter for *Jus Suffragii* addressed 'to the Women of Germany and Austria' under the heading 'On Earth Peace, Goodwill towards Men'. It was signed by 100 women and, it would seem, one man – Gandhi. She said:

> The Christmas message sounds as mockery to a world at war, but those of us who wished and still wish for peace may surely offer a solemn greeting to those of you who feel as we do. Do not let us forget that our very anguish unites us, that we are passing together through the same experiences of pain and grief. Caught in the grip of terrible Circumstance what can we do? Tossed on this turbulent sea of human conflict, we can but moor ourselves to those calm shores whereon stand, like rocks those eternal verities – Love, Peace, Brotherhood ...

She prayed for peace:

> We urge that peace be made with appeal to wisdom and reason. Since in the last resort it is these which must decide the issues, can they begin too soon? ...
> Peace on earth has gone, may Christmas hasten that day ... [21]

Eleanor Hobhouse – Emily's cousin, Henry's* daughter – stayed with her that Christmas. She was a Red Cross nurse and had been in Belgium shortly after war began and from her, Emily was able to learn firsthand about conditions as she saw them there. Refugees had been arriving in England from Belgium, fleeing from German rule. Emily, who was always thinking up ideas, had written to her brother in September suggesting he contact their cousin Sir Charles Hobhouse, Paymaster General, with the idea that some of the empty boarding houses and hotels in health resorts could be used to house them at a fixed sum per week. [22]

Emily was also interested in the work being done for the relief of interned enemy aliens by Eleanor's brother Stephen, a Quaker convert. As strong as Emily in his beliefs, he was soon to be in trouble as a conscientious objector.

---

* Rt Hon. Henry Hobhouse PC, (MP, JP), 1854–1937, was head of Emily's branch of the Hobhouse clan. He was a Privy Councillor and MP for East Somerset 1885–1906. He was married to Margaret Potter whose intellectually gifted sisters included Kate Courtney and Beatrice Webb.

The year ended with Emily still trying to convert Leonard to the pacifist cause and hoping he would bring the *Manchester Guardian* in as well. She was constant in her belief that Germany would give way on moral grounds. Leonard, however, was not moved.[23]

3

1915

After Basil Thomson, the Scotland Yard Intelligence Chief, had investigated pacifist organisations in 1917, he felt that the Cabinet would be interested to know that the Fellowship of Reconciliation* had, among other things, suggested that: 'Miss Emily Hobhouse should carry literature to Italy.'[1] By then, Emily had become well known to Scotland Yard and carrying literature was probably against regulations.

In any case, in March Emily decided to make her annual journey to her winter home in Rome. Whether she carried leaflets or not, she must have welcomed the opportunity to be active. She worked for pacifism in Italy, helped no doubt by influential friends.

Before leaving she wrote to her friend Jan Smuts:

8th March 1915 Asquith calls us 'Sparrows twittering'; let him mock … Our work is intense; we rest not day or night. I hope in Switzerland and Italy to consolidate the women there … America has started a

---

* Thomson said the society was started by the Quakers as a religious movement to 'establish a world order based on love' which forbade the waging of war and called for a life service. It exists today in Britain and the United States and was, for some time, active in Germany.

huge 'Women's Peace Party' and with Jane Addams* as President is helping and will probably lead us ...

We believe not in narrow nationalism, but in inter-nationalism, the brotherhood of man, and we recognise no enemies; all humanity are our friends and our interests everywhere are one and the same ...

[Talking of moral rights, she said] England's greatest opportunity came to her last August ... *She let it go by*, and has for ever lost it. Those great moments come seldom, they can never be recalled ... So I mourn ...

[She thanked Smuts for telling her about de Wet] ... that you have decided to spare his life. I rejoice not merely for him, but because it would have made matters worse and worse and your own life not safe for a moment ...[2]

Before leaving London, Emily had attended a large women's meeting in the Caxton Hall where it was agreed to send delegates to an International Congress of Women in The Hague, Netherlands in April. (The idea for this Congress of Women came about through the international suffrage movement, a meeting of which had been scheduled for Berlin in 1915. The Hague venue was the idea of Dr Aletta Jacobs, President of the Dutch National Society for Women Suffrage and Committee for International Affairs.**)[3]

On 9 April 1915 Emily wrote from Rome to Jane Addams in America.[4] Jane had agreed to chair The Hague Congress and she invited Emily as a delegate:

My dear Miss Addams,

Your letter of March 25th has just reached me. I feel honoured and deeply touched at your desire and that of the American delegates that I should be present at The Hague. You are right in supposing that I have from the first been associated with the movement. Since October I have worked at nothing else – for from the outbreak of war I have had it strongly in mind that Women must speak out and

---

* A long-time and highly respected social worker and peace activist in the United States, who became a member of the Quakers.
** Individual women or women from mixed societies could attend by expressing support for the Pacific Settlement of International Disputes and extension of suffrage to women.

pave the way to stop this horrifying war by creating an atmosphere of Peacefulness and international Sisterhood.

My whole heart and spirit are with you all at The Hague – Not to be there in body is a sore trial, but I am an invalid and in the cold north very incapacitated. Here in the warmth I can do a little, and am working amongst Italian women urging them to send written adherence (to the ideals of the Congress) even if a delegation is impossible. They are in an awkward position since their Govt is so undecided and, though personally I think it very unlikely, they fear War might be declared and they would be unable to travel back thro' Germany. If I could have got a permit to reach The Hague thro' Germany I would even now try to throw prudence to the winds and do so, but I fear there is not a ghost of a chance of such a favour – even if I knew how to apply. Passports, expense, lack of health all mitigate against me.

I look forward to a powerful and moving utterance from the women assembled – and I cannot believe other than that their courage, determination, and lofty spirit will be rewarded by some very real, if unrecognized, influence upon the govts of their countries.

May I put before you another point? I have been for years a student of the effect of war upon non-Combatants and have been collecting and want to collect a mass of evidence to shew [sic] that their Sufferings are far worse than that endured by soldiers.

I am trying to get permission to study this on the spot for in the warm weather I can do a little even in the north. But Americans could move freely. Could any of your delegation get to East Prussia and Poland and see for themselves – A high authority here tells me 2600 little children have died of starvation in one district only of Galicia – the total must be stupendous.

A thought has occurred to me since beginning this letter – viz that possibly the USA Ambassador here in Rome might – if I show him your letter – use his influence to get me a pass for The Hague. I will think of it.

Meanwhile pray believe that I watch every phase of the Women's Movement with deepest interest – but I am cut off from news by the Censorship unless it is sent me direct from Holland …

And on 21 April 1915 she wrote that she had done all she could by trying both the American Ambassador and the German Embassy to see if she could receive a permit to go to The Hague overland but had failed.[5]

The Women's Congress

The Congress was held in The Hague from 28 April to 1 May 1915. Twelve countries were represented. Only three women were able to get there from Britain. 180 women had applied for passports; most were turned down and the Admiralty refused passage to the rest. No French women were allowed to attend. (The final tally of representatives showed Austria 6, Belgium 5, Canada 2, Denmark 6, Germany 28, Great Britain 3, Hungary 10, Italy 1, Netherlands 1,000, Norway 12, Sweden 16, USA 47.)

The Resolutions included: 'a general protest against the madness and horror of war, and that peace negotiations should begin'.

In defining the principles for permanent peace, delegates had stated that women should share all civil and political rights and responsibilities on the same terms as men; that there should be open diplomacy and democratic control over foreign policy; that there should be no transfer of territory without the consent of the inhabitants; and that there should be self-determination by all peoples. They stated they believed in disarmament, freedom of the seas, free trade; that the investments of capitalists of one nation in the resources of another should be wholly at the risk of the investor, and they urged that all nations refer future international disputes to arbitration and conciliation. These were all objectives on which Emily would have agreed.

The Congress created an organisation for the future calling itself the International Committee of Women for Permanent Peace, which was later changed to the Women's International League for Peace and Freedom. Its headquarters was in Amsterdam and it had an executive committee consisting of a maximum of five women from each participating nation. Jane Addams was elected chair, Dr Aletta Jacobs and Rosika Schwimmer vice chairs and Chrystal Macmillan* secretary.

On the final day Rosika Schwimmer had moved that delegates appointed by the Congress should personally present the women's resolutions to the premiers and foreign ministers in the major European belligerent and neutral capitals and also to the President of the United States.[6] This was

---

* Chrystal Macmillan was one of the earliest women graduates from Edinburgh University, with second-class honours in moral philosophy and logic, and first-class honours in mathematics and natural philosophy. She was devoted to the cause of peace and justice for women of all classes and, when enabled in the 1920s, became a barrister to pursue these aims in the courts.

undertaken and when Jane Addams and Aletta Jacobs were in Rome they would have met with Emily and asked her to come to Amsterdam in the summer to help with the work.

Meanwhile, Emily's pacifist efforts had not gone unnoticed for Sir Rennell Rodd, the British Ambassador in Rome, wrote to the British Foreign Office on 18 June 1915 to complain. In a handwritten letter he said: 'It would much better for these people to stay at home' and added: 'It is Miss Emily Hobhouse I mean.'[7]

While the British Foreign Office was thinking about Emily, she had moved up to Milan where she said she had 'some long talks with their delegate, Rosa Genoni – who is gathering a band of peace workers "silently"'.

Italy entered the war on the Allied side on 15 May 1915.

Switzerland

On 5 July 1915 Emily wrote to Jane Addams from Berne:[8]

I halted here in Switzerland, whence I write, to rest on my way from Rome to join Dr. Jacobs [in Amsterdam] and have had the opportunity at Berne of talking with Germans, notably Baron Von Romberg the Minister at the German Legation. It was a great relief talking things out with him – and I wanted to tell you of it, because again from him I learnt that what has gone deepest into the German heart is our Food Blockade.**

He reiterated that Germany would only too gladly withdraw her submarine warfare on mercantiles if we would withdraw our Food Blockade. He told me they hated it [their submarine warfare] but could find absolutely no other way of replying to it. My idea [is] that England – as a step back towards the Civilization she upholds by word – should announce her decision to withdraw the blockade, wh would 'draw out the sting' as nothing else would do and pave the way for better things. I told him how jealous I was that my own country

---

** In his book *All the Way* Lord Robert Cecil, Viscount Cecil of Chelwood, the minister in charge of the blockade, explained that in olden times towns were blockaded in order to prevent commerce with other places. He said: 'This was not possible in this instance but Britain could and did interfere with Germany's overseas trade so that supplies could not get there through neutral countries.'[9]

should be the foremost in such a deed – but if she would not, even if pressed by President Wilson, then would not Germany take the moral lead. He replied that he thought Germany had already done so by telling America publicly that she was willing and ready to do so the day England withdrew her blockade. That of course is true, but is a dependant promise and not an act standing alone.

Do use your eloquence in putting before yr President this thought – that he should bring pressure on England to withdraw her blockade as an act of Return to Civilization …

[On small countries suffering through being forbidden to trade with Germany] … Is this fighting for the freedom of little nationalities? …

[About her own movements, Emily said she felt the journey round by London to Holland so difficult that under advice she applied to Romberg for a permit to pass overland] … He was so kind and thought it possible that I was persuaded into delivering my precious passports into his hand to go to Berlin for inspection and they have not come back yet, nor any response – so I am a prisoner here till they come …

[She was short of money and felt she was disappointing Dr. Jacobs] … Still I have used the time here by seeing many people – and getting in touch with the various Peace parties … However most of the Peace Societies don't want peace – they want Victory. On the whole I find a marked improvement of feeling since I was here in March, a shaking of the dry bones which gives one some hope …

Holland

As soon as possible Emily was off to Holland. She was unable to go through Germany but went through London without too much difficulty.

The British Foreign Office was anxious to stop her but was far too slow. It was not until 2 August they wrote to their various embassies and legations in France, Italy and Switzerland to ask them to apprehend her and send her straight back to England. It was Sir Rennell Rodd (from Rome) who told them he believed Emily was in Holland – 'but her maid is still here so perhaps that means she will return'.[10]

The clash of ideologies was inevitable. Britain was in the midst of a terrible war against a formidable enemy. Emily believed in peace, that all humanity was basically alike and she recognised no boundaries. Consequently she did not see anything wrong in talking to the German Ambassador nor in making attempts to resolve the issue.

On 26 July 1915 Emily wrote to Ambassador Romberg from Amsterdam thanking him for sending the reports, which she had given to Lord Bryce. She said: 'We are hard at work here – at the all-absorbing cause and we should feel rewarded if we could shorten the massacre by one day or one hour.'[11]

Again we pass to the introduction of **Emily's Journal**:[12]

In this war I have lived amongst the peoples of England, Italy, Switzerland, Holland, Germany, Belgium and France so I have had unusual means of observation. In each country the peoples are suffering and not one of them knew any ill of the people they are sent to fight against, hatred where it exists has been carefully planted and continually nourished by lies – left alone the peoples are not bellicose, understand the human feelings of other nations and if brought together make friends like soldiers in the trenches. That they should be made to go and hate, maim, and kill each other is more than pathetic; it is wicked.

Feeling this way strongly I wanted from the first to find means to tell the peoples (Germans, Austrians and Turks etc.) that amongst us there were many who did not hate them but held the principle of internationalism politically, and brotherly love religiously. I wanted, as far as one individual may, to begin laying the foundations of international life, even while the war was in progress – to say 'Here I come alone of my own free will into your country to bear you, even while our Governments are at war, a message of peace and Goodwill. Though alas! I am not a harbinger of Peace itself yet hope I am a harbinger of the Spirit of Peace. The first year, through ill-health, all I could do was to write a Xmas Letter of Goodwill to our Sisters in Enemy Countries and this was signed by a number of prominent women. It did not satisfy me, nor did the appeal I wrote to the 'Friends of Humanity' in America – more and more I felt that I must in my own person go to Germany.

In the Spring of 1915 when in Rome I obtained an interview with Prince von Schomberg, Austrian Ambassador to the Vatican, in order to tell him my views and desire to go to Galicia to investigate the sufferings of the population there and take them relief. He was sympathetic and promised to put my request before Vienna. He did so and all was going well when war broke out between Italy and Austria breaking the correspondence, necessitating his departure from Rome, and destroying my plan.

It was as well, for still I was not really strong enough. That summer I worked over three months in Amsterdam at the Women's International Bureau and this brought me into touch with many international women of broad minds and sympathies.

When passing thru' Switzerland I had spent a week in Berne and made the acquaintance of Baron von Romberg the German Minister there. He had given me a set of the German White books to send to Lord Bryce giving the other side of the 'Atrocity Stories' so widely read in his Report. He was extremely grateful to me for sending them because Lord Bryce's report had been extremely – indeed wholly one-sided though issued by a Commission of 'Investigation' – so-called. I may say here that Lord Bryce in writing to me admitted that he was unaware that the Germans had issued any Reports and yet they were easy to procure in any neutral nation! It was a deep regret and shame to me that Lord Bryce even after reading them all and circulating them amongst his Commission took no public steps to make known under his name and influence that there was at least another side to these stories.

Shortly after Emily reached Amsterdam, Dr Jacobs left for America; Rosika Schwimmer and Chrystal Macmillan both decided to follow her. This left Emily to manage the office the best she could. She had to pull together the Report of the Congress for publication. She wrote the foreword for it, in which she described the beginning of the movement:[13]

Foreword to Women's Congress Report

However silent and unseen, a movement must be wide and deep before it can find expression … From the very moment of the declaration of War … the germ of the idea, nameless and unformed, that the women of the world must come to the world's aid, was silently and spontaneously conceived ... In several countries, even belligerent – the work of peace and international fraternity received extraordinary impetus from the early days of the war.

The work was carried out in public and in private by individuals and groups, rarely by existing societies, but by new movements large and small, which arose simultaneously in many countries. The Union of Democratic Control* in London led the way, shortly followed by the Anti-Oorlog Rand in Holland, the Fellowship of Reconciliation in England, and the great Women's Peace Party in America; Germans formed the Bund Neues Vaterland; a great movement of peace swept through the women of Sweden; and later the Union Mondiale de la Femme arose in Switzerland. Many other organisations, some composed of men and women, some of women only, were formed throughout the world ...

Isolated individual women in various countries strove for clearer expression, and aided by Jus Suffragii, the Labour Leader, Vorwaerts, and a few kindred publications, found means to communicate with women in hostile lands. In the first month of the war Rosika Schwimmer outlined a scheme for a conference of neutrals for mediation, and went to the United States to enlist help and sympathy.... A number of prominent women signed my Letter of Christmas greeting to the Women of Germany and Austria and cordial and touching replies were received from both countries, amongst these was the Call to the Women of Europe by Lida Gustava Heymann of Germany. Socialist women meeting in Berne had issued a Peace Manifesto, widely published.

Emily continued in saying that the International Suffrage Alliance had been training women for years to work with each other. She praised Aletta Jacobs for concentrating and shaping the 'ardent yearning' of women of all lands for peace and justice. She talked of her wisdom and faith in sending out the 'call': 'Thus the Women's Congress unfurled the white flag of Peace and – despite ridicule, disdain, opposition, and disbelief – held it aloft before a blood-stained world.' She pointed out that: 'Peace is the eternal, the fundamental, the desirable. Hers is the vital principle of Love and before her

---

* The Union of Democratic Control was formed by those who dissented from British government policy, especially MPs, 5 August 1914. Members were ardent proponents of a negotiated peace.

outraged wrath war and its hatred must ultimately cower. Women, chief sufferers from war's curse, must vow that it shall never again usurp control.'[14]

Emily wrote Leonard a long letter on 31 August for his birthday and wondered whether he and his family would have a picnic with blackberry pasties and [clotted] cream where they were in Cornwall. Her body longed to be with them at Bude in Cornwall.[15]

She told him the Dutch ladies were all very kind to her and though she had to work in the office from 9 a.m. to 5 p.m., they made her very comfortable:

> As our Envoys are now all in America the whole responsibility is upon me here at present. The work is of exceeding interest and value and one day I think the World will own the fact … Now what we women want is peace not victory − *toute autre chose*. We want to get rid of the exploded idea of peace viz. that the Victor should dictate terms to the Vanquished. As all have some right and some wrong it is obvious that − to meet and settle it amicably is the wise and sensible plan and that it is worse than foolish to shed another drop of blood over it …

She noted that *The Spectator* had said Leonard had changed sides politically. She said she had bet him − a box of dates − years ago that he would change his stripes and now kidded that she wanted her due! But Leonard answered her by saying:

> I have not changed my principles or my party … I changed my view of the character of the German Govt and its ambitions, being impelled to this change by careful observation of the facts. We get plenty of the German side of the case (at the Manchester Guardian). I should not agree with you that is a 'dispute' where both sides have some right and some wrong. It is in our view a deliberate attack on the nations of Europe wh we have to ward off as well as we can …[16]

Leonard's book *The World in Conflict* was now out. Emily said: 'I do not know what the lines of your book may be, but roughly the above would be my argument if I were to venture to write.'

Emily was working hard trying to get funds for the overhead expenses of the International Committee. She mentioned this in a letter to Romberg in Berne, 1 September 1915, thanking him for a note of encouragement.[17] She attached their press release with a proposal for a Conference of Neutral Nations which should, without delay, offer continuous mediation: 'The work of the Conference should be to formulate concrete proposals of possible terms for peace as a basis for suggestions and objections on the part of the belligerent Governments and for public discussion.' They would continue until the belligerent themselves found sufficient common ground to meet for the final settlement of the peace treaty. It is not clear that Emily drafted the press release but it seems likely. On the notepaper Emily was listed as 'Acting Secretary pro tem'.

On 4 October 1915 Emily wrote to Jane Addams saying they were sending by hand some copies of the Report, an early edition, without the French and German sections which were not ready. Emily said she felt they should have a German woman and a French woman either in the office or closely connected with it to deal properly and internationally with their points of view and with those languages. They had had the first news from Aletta Jacobs and were very sorry to hear that Jane was ill.[18]

Meanwhile on their American trip Rosika Schwimmer had an amazing idea. Through Louis Lochner, a peace activist from Chicago who had acted as Jane Addams' secretary at The Hague, she was in touch with Henry Ford, the beloved car manufacturer. Out of this, and subsequent meetings, Henry Ford agreed to finance a ship, which would sail to Europe on a peace mission.[19]

Ford decided to sail in December on his *Peace Ship* for Scandinavia. Rosika Schwimmer and other activists would be on board. Only illness prevented Jane Addams from coming to Europe in the same way.[20]

4

HARD KNOCKS

Emily said it was for personal financial reasons she had to leave Holland on 24 October 1915. Aletta Jacobs had returned from America only the day before, so they just met. The British Foreign Office, which had found out when she was due, asked for a representative from Scotland Yard to meet and interview her at Tilbury Docks. Emily said she laughed off the 'strip search' that she had to undergo but it must have been unnerving.[1] Scotland Yard soon lost interest in her.

Emily spent six days in London, during which time she met old friends and saw some members of the [British] Committee for Permanent Peace. These members were not pleased she had been in the office in Amsterdam.

Emily told Jane Addams on 4 November 1915 that she knew they disliked her:

… my public self, my private self is unknown to them and objected to my name being at all prominent in this work, but I was hardly prepared for such an attitude as that wh I have encountered. All this does not matter to me privately, but my public self is affronted and I think rightly since my public actions, if they have meant anything, have meant a stand for the very principles embodied in many of our Resolutions. No other woman in England has so stood for those principles publicly and for that reason alone it has seemed to me that an association formed to propagate them should support and welcome me and not oppose my work.

But the Committee here has fallen into the hands of a clique – who were reared under the re-actionary influence of Mrs Fawcett and timidity and expediency prevail ... It has been a real revelation of narrowness. I have asked them to strike my name off the list of their association – but I want you to know and to let Dr. Jacobs know that this step does not mean that I withdraw from the work. I am at your disposal and hers, as far as my limitations of bodily strength and means permit – and there is no cause to which I am more willing to devote my life. I am thankful that I am so much stronger than I have been ... I realise that with this strong current against me, there may be no place that I can fill, but I can work a good deal outside ...

[She was glad to be alone by the sea in a quiet spot – probably Bude, Cornwall – saying her life had been spent so much alone that long stretches of solitude had become] a necessity in which to gather strength ...

[She wanted to get rid of her house in Cornwall and also her flat in Rome] One longs to possess *nothing* and so to be free for the service of humanity. Yet a woman so needs a home ... One is dragged two ways ...

[As a postscript] It is a real regret to me that they have elected such an unrepresentative five [The five women for the Permanent Peace Executive]. One is to be Irish, that is good, and Margaret Bondfield is splendid – but instead of three of one type all representing the NUWSS [National Union of Women's Suffrage Societies] we needed a strong brain like Vernon Lee [author, internationalist and musician] – and certainly a member of the Society of Friends – a woman of the standing of Margery Fry with broad cultivated mind and then one NUWSS would have completed it.[2]

Aletta Jacobs told Jane Addams on 4 December that the British Committee did not approve of Emily being in the office and treated her in such a way that she had withdrawn as a member of the British Committee and had asked to be an international member – as had some other British women, but it would have to be discussed.[3] It was suggested, not by Aletta Jacobs, that the delay in getting their overseas mail was due to Emily being in the office. This seems unlikely.

Emily was anxious to get back to Rome. It was Sir John Simon, the Home Office chief*, who asked the Permit Office to provide her with the necessary permit. He told Lord Robert Cecil on 28 October 1915 that he had decided not to detain her in Britain as he had no details of her conduct in Italy 'that would warrant such a measure. If the Italian authorities found her "presence obnoxious" it was up to them to forbid her return.' To which Cecil replied 8 November: 'The possibility of a woman known to have indulged in absurd and undesirable conduct in the past repeating this behaviour to the prejudice of British interests in Italy (or any other foreign country really) at a time when our relations with Italy are a matter of concern.'[4] However, the Foreign Office, who had time on their side, took no action.

On 10 December 1915 Jan Smuts wrote to Emily:

> I suppose this is the saddest Christmas that Europe has seen since the Black Death devastated Europe in the Middle Ages. What is going to become of us and our civilisation. I see no sign of decided victory on either side and it is apparently going to be a process of attrition which will leave Europe broken and finished at the end … We are letting out most of the rebel prisoners and de Wet will also get the option to go, but I don't think he will until every one is let go, which of course we cannot yet do …
>
> [The rains were good and everything looked like a garden. The Imperial Government had offered him the command in German East Africa but he had declined, feeling the Union wasn't quite safe at the moment] Goodbye my dear Auntie … Let me sometimes hear from you please.[5]

Switzerland

Emily had arrived in Switzerland, via France, in the first week of December.

A somewhat sorrowful Emily wrote to Aletta Jacobs from Berne, 7 December 1915:

---

* Sir John Simon later held the posts of Chancellor of the Exchequer and Foreign Secretary. He was a renowned chess player.

Dear Friend,

I write to you privately what I believe I am desired to tell you – a note to the Office with which of course I have no further connection, unless someday I shall learn that individuals may affiliate, (also I hope Societies) direct to the Central (Bureau).

From here I can write more freely, but you cannot reply because I leave for Rome via Milan in two days, and not only is the state of affairs in France and Italy very bad for us, but I personally am under surveillance. Particularly are they suspicious of anyone who passes thro' Switzerland and indeed if I linger here I shall not be allowed to cross the Italian frontier. I underwent a very long exam at the French border yesterday morning, but as I had nothing to hide and nothing to fear I did not mind, but the serious thing is they were expecting me.

Paris is full of unpleasant people, of that kind that always come to the surface in time of war. Our poor friends there are going thro' evil days, and ask me to put you *au courant*. The police have raided the Office in Rue Foudary and her private house (three men coming before 7 a.m.) also their printer's house. The Correspondence with your Bureau was seized, though not all. Every paper in Paris had articles and paragraphs about them during the successive days ... They are held up to the scorn and derision of the entire country in a blaze of most unenviable notoriety ...

[There followed changes of address and a request that the greatest prudence 'is taken on what is sent', followed by remarks on French politics] ...

I send you 50 francs – This is a gift for us from the Frenchman whose name is on the wall list with a 'le' before it. You must send no receipt, or write or post to him anything more. His name is **not** to appear in any list – put Anonymous (French) 50 frs. His wife came to me (he is in the South) it would be certain death for him ...[6]

As for Emily, her troubles had not ceased. The British minister in Berne, Evelyn Grant Duff, was evidently anxious to appear efficient – he had an extremely efficient wife who was organising a major food parcels scheme for prisoners of war in Germany and later became a Dame of the British Empire. He remembered that the Foreign Office had asked in August for Emily to be apprehended and sent back to England so he wired the Foreign Office for instructions.

Emily wrote to Aletta Jacobs on 8 December: 'I was writing you a long letter but that must wait a day or two.' She said she had been held up – 'no reason given' – and she wasn't certain whether it was a personal or general order: 'No hint was given me that I should be kept a prisoner in Switzerland – where it is high and cold … I have been advised to appeal direct to Sir Ed Grey …'[7]

She had wired accordingly to Arthur Ponsonby, Henry Hobhouse and Lord Courtney asking them to put pressure on the Foreign Office to let her continue her journey.

To Arthur Ponsonby MP she wrote:

> Please see Sir Edward Grey on my behalf. Ask him to instruct Legation Berne let me proceed to Rome. Passports self and maid in order, viséd London and Paris for Italy via Switzerland. Resting here two days, find myself stopped no reason assigned. Health weak must go on. Must wind up affairs in Rome cannot afford to keep flat there longer nor stay here.[8]

Finally Cecil relented and by 22 December authorised Grant Duff to give Emily a visa provided she promised not to indulge in propaganda, especially peace propaganda.[9]

Grant Duff tried to get Emily to take an oath, which she would not, but she had to sign a paper:

> I the undersigned, Emily Hobhouse, hereby solemnly and sincerely declare that if I receive the British visa to proceed to Italy, I undertake not to indulge in propaganda of any sort, especially propaganda in favour of peace, and not to remain in Italy any longer time than is necessary to settle my personal affairs. In making this declaration I clearly understand that it is open to the Italian authorities to refuse me permission to enter Italy if they judge fit.

The declaration was duly signed and witnessed.[10]

Four days later Emily wrote to Aletta:

> One last letter to you as I leave Switzerland and descend into what will be like the silence of the grave.

My telegram reached London because a wire came from the Foreign Office reversing the orders of Grant Duff the British Minister at this Legation. He however, to save his dignity I fancy, said I was to take an oath that 'I would do no peace propaganda of any sort or kind in Italy'. I refused to take an oath – and so was made to sign a declaration of the same words … The Italian Consul made not the slightest difficulty and so off I go, and I do not envy myself the experience, for I shall be under close surveillance … and very likely my flat will be raided before I get there … I have arranged to send news if possible to Gertrud Woker and if you wish to write to me that also would be the best way, putting on your envelope to her Via Deutschland … She promises to be my private censor … Please, please no word of Peace. I should not at all mind an English prison, but draw the line at an Italian ditto! …

[As compensation to being kept in Switzerland she said she had met many of the Swiss women interested in peace – but found that even the nicest wouldn't work easily with each other unless they agreed on every point.] I think the younger section … are shaking themselves free of the older suffragist … There are others too, anxious to start a general popular agitation to shew that the people insist on some effort being made by this country for peace. I do hope that Mr. Ford is really coming, he and his party might do something to unite and give expression to these various parties….

The accounts I have of Italy are very sad. I hate going there.

She gave the names of the five for the Executive from France which she hoped she got right as she hadn't been able to (was afraid to) write anything down.[11]

Italy

It was Chrystal Macmillan who answered Emily, writing to thank her for all she had done in Amsterdam.[12] Chrystal said she was very sorry to hear in London the way some people had behaved and told her: 'You will be glad to know that we have had letters from one of the women you wrote to in Uruguay and from one in Japan – very friendly both.' She remarked that the women in Manitoba had got full suffrage and it was expected in Alberta soon.

Perhaps unbeknown to Emily – she does not mention it – British Prime Minister Asquith paid a visit to Rome at the end of March. During this visit he saw Pope Benedict XV. In his memoirs, Asquith said: 'Our talk was naturally confined to the war and germane topics: the Pope carefully refraining from indicating any leaning of his own to either side, and I giving no encouragement to a feeler which he incidentally threw out that he might act as mediator.'[13] In fact Asquith took the cavalier stand, so admirable in the British if one is not concerned about loss of life.

Emily concluded her affairs and left Italy in April 1916.

Switzerland Again

She wrote to Aletta Jacobs on Easter Day, 23 April 1916, from Berne that she was saddened by the thought that just when their work was most needed, the Bureau seemed to be breaking down.[14]

Aletta had wanted her to go back to Holland but Emily said that it was impossible for several reasons: the English committee were dead against her being there; it was known that Chrystal Macmillan could only work with 'machinelike subordinates'; her own bad health necessitated her keeping very warm; and getting a permit was expensive and impossible. She told Aletta she felt inclined to join the Ford Commission if it could get the free passport facilities which it had asked for. It was her hope that the International Bureau and the Ford Commission would work together.

She also told Aletta of the work of Rosa Genoni in Milan, who she felt was very brave to have had an appeal printed privately and spread amongst the crowd on May Day, and of the Italian women of Zurich who were being organised to do the same. Emily said she had written the Zurich people a little greeting and suggested that they should revive the old custom of choosing 'Peace' for the Queen of May, and should carry the symbolic figure through the streets of the city.

Although in her Journal Emily tells us some of the things she was doing she omitted to mention that she, along with forty-three delegates representing socialist parties in eight countries, attended the Socialist Conference at the little alpine village of Kienthal, known as the Second Zimmerwald Conference.[15] These radical Socialist Conferences were organised by

Robert Grimm, a Swiss Deputy, with the idea of replacing the annual meetings of the Socialist Second International that had been cancelled because of the war and were meant to be in the cause of peace. Such representatives of European socialist parties as could get to Switzerland attended. No one could come from Britain but both Lenin and Trotsky were at the first conference and Lenin at the second. It was at these conferences that Lenin propounded his revolutionary theory and this caused a split. His caucus was referred to as the Zimmerwald Left; Grimm and the majority were referred to as the Zimmerwald Centre. Emily was there as an observer and boldly signed the register as such.

5

PRELUDE TO THE
JOURNEY

On returning from Kienthal, Emily addressed a propaganda rally organised by the Berne International Union for Permanent Peace. It was reported in the Swiss newspaper *Der Bund* that she had reviewed the Peace Resolutions of The Hague Women's Congress.[1] When Evelyn Grant Duff, the British Minister, read this report under the title *Die Frauen und der Friede* [Women and Peace], he was furious. He told the Foreign Office Emily had breached her signed declaration (Emily understood this paper was only for Italy, and, for once, some at the Foreign Office agreed). Should he revoke her passport? he asked. He said that peace propaganda at the present time was 'open disloyalty.'[2]

Emily was now labelled in the Foreign Office, perhaps fairly for once, as a 'peace crank'. 'Perhaps,' it argued, 'by revoking her passport she would leave Switzerland and she might be frightened into silence ...' After twenty-four days, on 27 May 1916 British Foreign Secretary Grey authorised Grant Duff to withdraw Emily's passport.[3]

However, by this time Emily was working on a new project. She had seen an article in *The Times* (which was available in every country, even during the war) about Ruhleben, the British civilian internees camp outside Berlin, and she thought she would very much like to go to see it, and she would also like to go to Belgium to see conditions there for herself. With this in mind she approached the German Ambassador, Romberg. He was sympathetic and we know from the German records that he went to the very top – to Chancellor Bethmann Hollweg – to ask for permission.[4]

It took a long time to get a reply. Emily fretted away her time at Gunten, a mountain resort near Berne, writing letters to the German Embassy to keep the matter in mind. In the end she was permitted to go to Belgium but denied permission to go to the internment camp. However, Romberg advised her to apply again when in Brussels as he knew the man in charge would be sympathetic.[5]

Grant Duff, meanwhile, was having difficulty locating Emily as the Swiss police were forbidden to give out the addresses of foreigners. On 5 June his staff at last managed to find her. He then sent Emily what he called a 'casual' message requesting her to call at the Legation on an unspecified morning. He told the Foreign Office that he made the message deliberately vague 'so as not to arouse her suspicion'.[6]

Emily was not deceived. She wrote in her **Journal**:[7]

Thus in the summer of this year 1916 on finding myself again in Berne I called on von Romberg and with my vision ever in my mind's depths that I must go to Germany. I suddenly, while sitting in his room, saw in his face my opened door. To a man so sympathetic and broadminded as Baron von Romberg it was easy to explain my feelings and points of view and bit-by-bit I carried him with me. Yet I shall never forget his start as of a new light penetrating his mind when I said to him 'I have no Enemies.' It was evident that he made up his mind that I should go – and promised his influence with Berlin.

It took time, and patience on my part was necessary awaiting the reply – he himself in a visit to Berlin pleaded my cause. My request was grounded on an immediate desire to learn the truth in the interests of humanity and peace – and on larger issues to accentuate the fact of the brotherhood of mankind – the highest internationalism – Christian love and amity – to accentuate this as unalterable in the darkest moment of the World's history. I know that he 'understood' and that his personal sympathy and high-minded belief in my Mission prevailed and gained me the end I so desired. Particularly I asked to study the condition of non-combatants in Belgium, our Civilians in Ruhleben, and the food supply in Germany and its effects on Women and Children.

But time had elapsed and I waited a good month at Gunten and Berne in suspense often so weak and ill that I hoped with my body a refusal would come, though my mind and spirit knew it would be 'Yes'. And one evening, late, the letter come which I knew would settle it. I was still weak and ill and so shrank from the physical effort and strain that must be involved that for full half an hour I let the letter lie unopened. With my weak heart and difficulty of bearing any agitation I first went to bed feeling that only there in complete repose could I face the news. I was a great coward that night. Herr Schubert, (1st Secy) wrote so kindly to tell me the 'good news' and there I lay in terror of what might lie before me in Germany physically – afterwards at home morally. I faced the bare fact that I had foreseen and longed for, for a year and nine months and I shrank from it.

The conditions had not come and that meant still further delay. During this period came Mr Grant Duff's letter, the British Minister, commanding my presence at the Embassy. I knew that answers to the queries he would make would involve disclosure of my plan to which he (with no right) would be averse, and that therefore I must go at once or not at all. Therefore I hurried down to von Romberg and explained the position which he, fully aware of Grant Duff's idiosyncrasies, wholly understood and my passport (a humanitarian one) was made out and given to me and I was told the conditions were come and that I was to go to Belgium and be handed over to an Official at the border ...

6

Emily's Journal: Wartime Journey across Germany

We now get to an interesting part of Emily's Journal.[1] The Journal records day-to-day events, but was written later. Although Emily had an excellent memory, she had to leave her notebooks in Switzerland or they would have been confiscated. They are not preserved with her papers:

We were in a hurry because I must leave Berne in four hours to catch the train to Basel and I had to pack and make arrangements for Phoebe [the maid she had with her in Rome]. In the hurry therefore I was never told what 'conditions' of my visit Belgium were laid down and this might have made a difference in my plans had I known.

I was hastily introduced to young Von Rosenberg the courier who undertook to meet me next morning at Basel with the motor and I was directed to a quiet and unknown temperance Inn, the Blue Cross 'Blaukreizhaus' which lay in a quiet street. Here, after a wretched supper and a most fatiguing and agitating day I exhausted myself by diligently washing all labels off my bottles and pill-boxes, etc, not an easy task and as it turned out quite unnecessary in my case. I posted a letter in Berne before leaving, to Mr Grant Duff saying I had received his note but was leaving Berne for a trip – nevertheless 'Immediately on my return I shall have much pleasure in calling at the Embassy'.

[June 7th] Precisely – with German punctuality – at 7.20 a.m. as advised the Courier drove up to the Inn and found me with equal punctuality standing on the threshold with my bags and baskets. They hoisted them into the car and off we went through the empty streets to the barrier some 4km distant. First there was the Swiss Custom[s] which opened my things very perfunctorily and then the long wooden arm of a level crossing was lifted a little. I slipped under and lo! we were in Germany. In a moment of time one's whole mental orientation was changed. The foolishness of it all was startling. Nature had made no barrier – the earth and stones and grass were the same – one step only made the difference between the country of a friend and of an enemy! No barrier but man, or at least governments, had put up landmarks saying 'here is all mine, there is all yours. Our interests are different and each must look after his own!' But nature had made no barrier – a long level road swept through a green meadowland on both sides the same and the people actually speaking the same language. As Borngräber [German playwright] says in his *Bergpredigt*: 'Away with frontiers, down with all landmarks. You on that side, you on this side – you are brothers and the World is your Fatherland.' To me it was a wonderful moment and I felt as in a dream.

Von Rosenberg, a nice youth, took my German phrase book and dictionary which I had begged leave to bring and with no sort of difficulty we passed the German Customs. The car slipped through and another kilometre or so slid by before we gained the little station now the terminus, for German trains no longer run into Basel – the line is cut. A wounded soldier with calm patient face was being carried in a stretcher and let up and down the platform in a baggage lift. I asked the same privilege – a wheeled chair was brought and I was pushed by genial German porters into the lift. Then they bought me a paper and we left for Cologne.

The first thing I saw on opening the paper was the death of Kitchener[*] and the loss of the *Hampshire*. A crowd of memories rushed back upon me and I felt regret that I should not be able to make him

---

[*] Emily had many dealings with Lord Kitchener when he was Commander-in-Chief of the British Army in South Africa during the Anglo-Boer War 1899–1902. In 1914 he was made Secretary of State for War with Cabinet rank.

learn (what however he knew well enough) that Belgium was not devastated and destroyed as he destroyed South Africa – the Free State and Transvaal. It was in any case a dramatic moment in which to have learnt of his death, and to the German mind I saw it meant a great deal. My opinion was that though no special military loss, Kitchener was a loss to peace-prospects being probably the only man in England who was impervious to public opinion and with shoulders broad enough to bear that hostile opinion if he thought we could gain no military decision and must make peace by negotiation.

(Before leaving Switzerland I left all papers, money and directions with Gertrude Woker of 17 Riedweg, Berne, where also a good deal remains till the war is ended. She came to see me off and to both her family and the Kochers I owe much help and sympathy. I should also like to record Baron von Romberg's thoughtful advice to me – his enemy – to consider well before going, lest afterwards it should compromise me in England. I took council on this point with my Swiss friends who all felt nothing but good would come of it.)

Von Rosenberg left me alone in my compartment – of which I was glad – the train ran very smoothly and did not shake me and I could lie down. The country looked so fair and green and peaceful and prosperous, it was hard to reconcile it with press accounts which have coloured [sic] all minds. Officials in spite of my English appearance, and few Anglicized German phrases, were all so genial, helpful and courteous and indeed during the whole of my stay I never encountered one word or look of discordance – distinctly the reverse. Yet I could not be and was not taken for an American.

We stopped at various large stations. Everywhere the people seemed busy and purposeful – cheerful and smiling (though no hilarity) but at the same time serious and calmly confident. There was no look of a beaten people nor of a people likely to be beaten. I wanted to buy the notorious War-bread** as a first step towards my study of the Food Question. I think it was at Offenburg that the opportunity came. A barrow at the station came down the line selling sandwiches, wines, mineral waters and such strawberries. I bought a large and substantial sandwich made of this bread and cheese – and some fruit. The sandwich cost half a mark, 6d [sixpence]. I usually give 4d [fourpence] in normal

---

** Joseph C. Grew, then Secretary at the American Embassy in Berlin, said: 'We have no white bread any more; it is brown and the flour is mixed with a specific percentage of potatoes, but it is not bad.'

times in England, for a ham sandwich half the size. To my astonishment I found the bread delicious and from there to the end of my visit I eat it and enjoy it thoroughly. It agreed with me perfectly, far better than the bread of Italy, Switzerland or the Westminster Palace Hotel.

At Wiesbaden we changed trains and had a good half hour so I invited Von Rosenberg to take tea with me. There were men waiters apparently robust and of military age. The tea was fairly good but no milk was provided, instead lemon was served. I asked for biscuits and a packet was brought and Von Rosenberg had spread bread and butter. The packet of biscuits lasted me a long time. The people looked well nourished. Our journey continued down the Rhine Valley that pretty, but I think over-rated scenery and so idealized by Turner. Fruit orchards bordered much of the way and the ripening cherries were being gathered by men and women, but chiefly women, with ladders against the trees. Here and there ex-soldiers (perhaps on leave) were working in the fields and once I saw a squad of men who were evidently prisoners-of-war also at work.

It must have been towards seven o'clock when the towers and spire of Cologne rose above the plain and we drew up in the great station crowded with soldiers, kindly looking solid men, their physique struck me as very superior to that of our slim, ill-grown Tommies *. I had a steep flight of steps to climb at the station exit and when at last we got outside there was no conveyance of any sort to take us to the hotel. We had to wait a full half hour and I was thankful to sit down on my campstool. Soldiers, railway men and children stood about the groups. The children looked a bit ragged and unkempt (for Germany), about 15 of them came round me and I distributed chocolate amongst them which I had brought from Berne. I doubt if they were very hungry because oddly enough few of them began at once to eat it as children usually do. I had to teach them to say '*Ich danke Ihnen*' for it, while the men standing about smiled genially. It was strange how calmly they took me, considering that young Von Rosenberg was not in uniform.

It was necessary to order a cab from some stables so the delay was considerable before at last we drove off. At the entrance of the old bridge (I think a drawbridge) and guarded, a soldier mounted the box of the cab and we walked the horse across to the farther side where the soldier left us. Cologne is a garrison town and full of military. Opposite the cathedral was a quiet small hotel to which he took me and selected for

---

* British soldiers

me a quiet but very comfortable room. Charming, well-mannered and very pretty chambermaids who said 'gnädige Frau' every other moment.

It was late, though still so light with our first experience of Summer Time, and I went down hungry to supper. I ordered soup and some rice pudding. It was my first experience too of short commons, for the good bowl of soup I expected turned out to be a wee cupful about the size of an after-lunch coffee cup. My inside felt distinctly aggrieved. But then usual three thinnish slices of bread were there and though no pudding appeared there was brought me a very few stewed cherries. So I went to bed while Von Rosenberg went to the town Commandant to explain my presence and assure him I should depart early next day. In Cologne, he said they were very particular, and I fancy they gave him some trouble there about me.

I had a nasty ending to a long strange day. In my bedroom there were double windows but I did not know it. The outer one had cross bars which showed, the inner had none which made it invisible. I went to look out and thrust my head forward precipitately to gain the window with bars which I could see. I came in very violent contact with the inner glass which was invisible. The blow fell on the bridge of my nose and how it escaped being broken I do not know. I was stunned for some time but just roused myself enough to recollect the brandy in my bag and I rubbed that well on the place. But the pain to the whole face and brow was great. I thought of how Mamma did the very same thing and how it brought on the malignant cancer between the bones of her brow and nose and caused an agonizing death.

[June 8th] Next morning I got down for my coffee at 7 o'clock and found a very excellent coffee and milk ample in supply and the same three large thin slices of bread and some preserve (I think no butter but my notes left in Berne will supply that point accurately). The bill was moderate, the hotel seemed well supplied with male waiters, etc. We walked to the station under the lovely cathedral which I longed to stop and lionize – someday.

Again the station (another one) was thronged with soldiery and I knew they were massing on the Western frontier. Again steps to climb, Continental stations are dreadful in that respect. A comfortable carriage and an easy run of some three hours – past Aachen – Aix-la-Chapelle (burial place of our far off ancestor Charlemagne) brought us to Heberstal, the Belgium frontier.

7

Emily's Journal: Into Belgium, June 1916

German troops had pushed through Belgium en route for France in August 1914. They had a million men in five armies and expected a quick victory. This had not happened. Their advance had been halted near the River Marne 30 miles (50km) from Paris, and after a battle they had been forced to retreat. The British had joined the French and both sides now resorted to trench warfare. Trenches, with underground bunkers, reached across France from Switzerland to the sea. It was there that the armies faced each other for four years.

Except for a small salient around Ypres, in the north-west, the whole of Belgium was occupied. Two German armies, with thousands of troops, remained in Belgium. It was reported that in 1914 where there had been the slightest resistance – even a single shot – retaliation had been severe; houses were burnt and hostages, including women and children, were taken and shot. The world was outraged and Emily, always sceptical of atrocity reports which were used extensively by the press for propaganda purposes, wanted to see these places for herself. Naturally she wanted to talk to the people but this was forbidden.

John Horne and Alan Kramer in their book *German Atrocities, 1914: A History of Denial* give us an idea of the extent of these atrocities. The first were reported at Liège which Emily only travelled through; then at

Aerschot where twenty captured Belgian troops were shot and thrown into the river after which burning and looting took place and men were rounded up and shot. In Dinant, which Emily was unable to visit because of the bad weather, things were worse. Women and children were shot and the whole town was torched. At Louvain the famous library, home of many medieval documents, was said to have been deliberately set on fire and completely destroyed, a fact omitted completely in the German White Paper, while the inhabitants were terrorised, their homes burnt and hostages shot. At Charleroi where civilians were said to have been used as human shields, house burning and executions took place.

Emily spent ten days in Belgium in June 1916 and visited many of these places as well as Brussels, Malines and Antwerp but, although she was allowed to travel wherever she wished, she was forbidden to talk to any of the inhabitants, a matter that she deeply regretted. Thus, although she understood the difficulties of living under martial law from her South African experience, she was prevented from fully comprehending the extent and brutality of the occupation.

The strength of Emily's testimony must be in what she saw with her eyes. She had been in Belgium in 1902, and again in 1904 when she had studied lace-making, and knew her way around so could compare the occupied country with its peacetime state.

We pick up **Emily's Journal** at the Belgium border:[1]

Here we changed trains and I had to wait in the Customs while Von Rosenberg went to look for the Escort sent from Brussels to meet me. Presently he came, looking rather sleepy and introduced himself as Baron Falkenhausen, Freiherr von Friedensthal. He was in uniform, though not of the picturesque kind. He wore a long pale blue military overcoat which did not become him very well as he is short – and has an ungainly walk. He never wore the beautiful cloak which falls in such classic and graceful folds. He was fair, clean shaven and very young looking – spoke English well and idiomatically and was full of merriment. I think his laughter was largely nervous. However we soon made friends and I was able to put him at his ease, though I think being escort to a formidable old maid in a grey bonnet and a golf cape (for it was very cold) was really rather alarming to him. He asked me how old I judged him to be and I said about my nephew's age or a little more – say 26. He said he was 32 and then spoke of a wife and child! Afterwards it all came out that they had married just a few weeks before war broke out (she is an Austrian-born Gräfin). His duty separated them and he had only seen her once since for a few days. She was at home at the family place in Silesia.

Von Rosenberg made his adieux – he had done service on the Russian frontier and had since travelled immensely (I think he told me as many miles as if he had been round the world). His father's castle was on the Russian frontier. He was used to catching trains waking up at all hours or never sleeping at all. He was about 22.

A few minutes and we were in Belgium entering it at a pretty part, wooded and hilly country. The first village we passed was Doulain or Dourrain. And it lay calm and lovely in the valley; but on the heights, wood crested above it, stood the ruins of what had been a fine villa which Falkenhausen pointed out to me. He said, 'There you see the first house destroyed in Belgium by the German Army.' Then he went on to explain that it was inhabited by a Belgium Count who determined to resist from his private house standing alone as it does, the passage of the German army. He barricaded the house and fired from windows and roof. It was naturally replied to and the result was a ruin. No other house in the vicinity seemed to be touched. I found as the days went on that this fact was characteristic of the destruction wherever I was brought in contact with it. One house would be in ruins, the other next door to it would be intact. One street in ruins, the next to it intact – one block in ruins, the surrounding blocks untouched, and so on.

We soon passed Liège where excepting about Herstal things seemed in status quo. One looked in vain for the famous fort, but learnt that modern forts are invisible. It is an ugly coal-mining town. The suburb Herstal was the scene of much street fighting and where the rougher element of the industrial population, factory women and children attacked the invaders and threw boiling water and oil from their windows upon them.

Then a thrill came over me as I neared Louvain [Leuven] and the gable of the Cathedral was pointed out to me. A pretty town with its river running through. From here onwards the scattered houses in the fields shewed signs now and again of the passage of the armies, for cottages shewed repairs of roof or wall but not by any means all of them, and fewer as we approached Brussels which we reached at midday. A good fourteen years since I was first in Brussels viz in the spring of 1902. I was there again in 1904 when I was studying lace-making. The town looked peaceful and lovely as usual, though of course a large number of German officers were in the streets as well as men. The railways were entirely manned by German officials (I learned later that the entire Belgian staff refused to serve). They, however, run their own trains and police their own streets and try their own civil cases in their own law courts. The Belgian police have, however, to salute German officers.

Talking of saluting, one of the clearest memories that will live with me of my whole tour is the 'eyes' of the German soldiery. It appears that in the German army a soldier must salute his superior not only with his hand but with his eyes. He must look straight into the Officers' faces with his eyes. Walking always in Belgium with an officer as I did I faced continually these eyes nominally saluting – really charged with deep, mingled, wonderful expressions. Eyes of all colours, blue, grey, brown, yellowish brown, black, hazel all made to look straight at you and all charged with feeling I find it hard to depict in words. One thing in common though I think all were tired – weary – trying but not always succeeding to hide their fatigue from the Superior – pathetic, pleading, gentle also for the most part – one or two with hatred – but not one fierce. Very often sad and also eyes as of men in physical pain – one or two only with youthful merriment. These constantly recurring glimpses into the inmost souls of scores of men moved me to tears and haunt and will haunt me for years.

Conditions: We drove straight to the hotel. In the train my Baron as I called him, told me he had arranged to take me to the Astoria and though it was delicately put, it was clearly enough conveyed to me that I had no choice in the matter. He also alluded to the conditions under which I had come – of which I was ignorant and they certainly came rather as a blow, because I had not been told them and, though prepared for rigid martial law, had hardly expected such strictness. He said I must go straight to Brussels and it would be necessary that I should always sleep there, that it was not considered advisable that I should speak to Belgians and that I was to be always accompanied by him. I expressed regret because, as I said, such rules would militate against any chance of real investigation, but there I was and of course I should loyally obey the rules laid down. On that point he need have no doubts. He replied they had perfect confidence in me, but these were the rules and no exception could be made.

Therefore I arrived at the Astoria feeling on parole – and also that I should be able to learn very little beyond which my eyes would teach me of the actual material destruction. In fact I said to my Baron: 'Your refusal to let me speak to Belgians is your greatest condemnation and in one way I learn more from the prohibition than all the people could tell me.'

The hotel was very weird and silent – several common rooms shut up. I had, however, a light cheerful room on the 4th floor for 5frs and with hot and cold taps in the room.

More Conditions: The manager was told that I was under the protection of the Political Department and I was told I must not go out into the street, not even to enter a shop or buy a stamp unless the Baron were with me. He took me to my room and left me to change and rest, asking that he might go back to change and dress as he had been up all night. He would come later to take me to the authorities.

Very soon I went down to get some tea, the restaurant dining room was dim and deserted, one waiter wandered forlornly about. I drank my tea and asked if I could have some boiled eggs for supper at 6 p.m. as I did not take late dinner. 'Ah', said the waiter with a dejected air '*Nous ne dinons jamais maintenant*' [We never dine now]. The hall was empty and no books or newspapers were anywhere to be seen. Only now and then an officer passed through, truly an hotel *mort*.

At 4.30 p.m. the Baron appeared much refreshed and we sallied forth – the evening was fine but cold. We took the tram and I noticed that he stood on the platform and would not come in and sit down amongst the people and this continued throughout my stay. I noticed at once the antagonistic looks of the people and he admitted that was the reason and that it was torture to him to be exposed to their insults – often silent ones. In fact as the days went on I saw that he kept entirely aloof – would never – at my suggestion – ask the way of a Belgian in the street, nor go with me if he could avoid it into a shop. He shrank. 'It serves you right,' I would say, 'You have no business here.' 'Still if we were not here, you would be', was his reply. And that I think was very probable.

The people also would look at me with wide-eyed curiosity, not able to understand how it could come about that a woman so evidently English could be going about with a German officer. I kept as grave as possible, and avoided his helping hand to alight from or climb into trams and sometimes they thought I was under arrest, sometimes I am sure they thought I was German too and their faces took the same look of antagonism. It was very disappointing that I could not talk to them at all as I longed to do.

This first afternoon we went to the beautiful house (formerly of some Belgian official) where the staff of the Political Department was installed. Baron von [der] Lancken*, Von Romberg's friend who had given me a letter to him, was unfortunately in Berlin so I only saw Count Harrach his deputy and young von Moltke who with Falkenhausen made up the Chiefs of that Department. As I could not go upstairs Count Harrach very kindly came down to see me in the very elegantly furnished Empire drawing room looking out upon the park – now closed to the public. Count Harrach is the son of a well-known German artist and is himself a sculptor residing mostly in Florence. He was handsome cultivated and highbred. He was a bit shy about his English but spoke it to please me, and now and then lapsing into French. Even the fact that he had to give me 'orders' and make me understand that I must strictly obey could not detract from his exceeding charm. He forbade my going into the war zones, but I was free to go where I pleased in the 'occupied zones'. I asked if it were not possible to get a car or some conveyance to move about from village to village etc, but he said no motor was available, I must use the trains and in any case always return to sleep in Brussels. With my limited time and powers I felt this would be a great drawback to the work I wanted to do. I spoke of my desire to go also to Berlin which he promised to forward. Then followed an informal and friendly talk with all the three men – von Moltke moved me immensely – such a very sweet almost boyish face and very tall. He is not married, but my Baron said he was as old as himself. We talked of the naval battle** and the war generally. They asked me what England was fighting for and why. And the vivid impression I carried away from those three men was their broken-hearted consternation that England should have declared war upon them in the darkest moment of their history.

---

* Baron von der Lancken was chief of the Political Department.
** The Battle of Jutland.

We took a little détour on returning to the hotel so as to see something of Brussels and arranged early to bed and to spend the first day quietly after so tiring a journey. I found it very cold. Reaching the hotel, I went to have my supper and found that the Baron intended to sit with me. This he did, ordering a drink – whiskey and soda – the reply being 'there was none', so something else was substituted. For supper came brown bread very similar to that in Germany but the three slices were large and thick instead of medium and thinnish, far more in fact than I wanted. The prices also of my meals were the same or if anything rather less than I pay in the Westminster Palace Hotel. The dejected waiter waited. During this meal we were able to talk and learn somewhat of each other's lives and points of view. Falkenhausen told me of his year spent at King's, Cambridge – of his English friends. Mr Wodehouse son of Lord Kimberley I think, and the Quickes of Devonshire – his grief that his friend Quicke had already been killed in the war. How he had valued his English friends and loved the English country life and hunted on Exmoor etc, how England's entry into the war with them had broken all his ideals. Interesting too, it was, to note in the light of the average English view that we are out to kill Prussianism, that he and his friends who had been attracted to and had embraced the English liberal and democratic views, had now definitely discarded them and returned to arguing that their bureaucratic system was after all superior.

After supper I pleaded for bed and he took me to the lift promising to call for me at 10 a.m. There is German time plus Summer Time in Belgium and I went to bed with the sun shining and read by daylight till nearly 11 p.m. I do not think I switched on the light once in either country.

Friday, June 9th The morning was cold, windy, fine and showery by turns. I rang to have my coffee in bed and it came up, good in quality plentiful in quantity and three very large thick slices of the delicious brown bread and plenty of good butter and jam. I could never eat more that a part of one slice of bread and kept also a piece for the afternoon, the rest went down again.

Punctually at 10 a.m. came my Baron and found me awaiting him in the gloomy silent hall. He suggested taking me to the lace depôt – set going by the Germans to provide work for the countless lacemakers in the country districts. The turnover is large and the profits

go to the Belgian Red Cross. I have in my Aide Mémoire* noted the
details about this work, which was evidently supported solely by the
German officers buying for their wives. Some of the lace was good,
but none of it the very first class, nor of the type I most admire. Also
the wages did not seem to me high enough, tho' undoubtedly a help.
I bought a couple of small bits as it seemed de rigueur. Just below was
another shop where blouses were being made, the manager being an
Americanized German. Some thirty young women make these and
work daily; in busy times several dozen more are employed. This of
course, was to show me what the Germans were doing and I quite felt
that whatever business they undertake they do well.

Coming out and wandering in what seemed a happy busy town,
we came with a sudden start on a queue of people, three or four deep,
mostly women and girls with a sprinkling of men – the Belgians
waiting to be fed. It was a sharp reminder of tragic facts. They were very
neat in appearance, quiet, orderly folk but the faces were strained and
wan. I watched, not liking to do it, and spoke a bit with the Baron over
it. (This is further described in an article I wrote about it.) He promised I should see something of these people and visit the Communal
Kitchens. Afterwards it became an ordinary sight and one that recurred
again and again in different quarters of the town and in different towns.
It always gave me a shock and brought one back to realities.

He suggested turning into the Cathedral which I was glad to
do, wondering if any ill had happened to it. Seeing all in statu quo
I exclaimed with delight that no harm had been done at which he
drew himself up and said stiffly, 'Germans do not destroy Cathedrals'.
And in the end I think this will be found to be true, Louvain Cathedral
and Malines are both partially injured (tho' Service is being held in
both) but the one, Malines was injured equally by the cannon of both
sides, and not much; the other, Louvain, caught fire accidentally, the
Germans doing their best to extinguish it. Dinant Church is, I believe,
destroyed as a result of the street fighting consequent upon the civilian
outbreak – and probably churches in the small towns of Visé etc but
we paid no respect to churches in South Africa. Rheims is the usual
instance, but the French used it as an observation post and not till then
did a German ball hit it and then only one. At least the 'White book'

---

* The Aide Mémoire and other papers were left with Gertrude Woker to be retrieved
after the war. They have not been found with Emily's papers.

on this must be read before judgment is formed. Anyhow grand old Brussels Cathedral stands unharmed and so does Antwerp. We admired the piers and the wonderful tints and hues of the stained glass.

Later we went to call on Captain Bruhn the singularly capable and genial chief of the department that works with and controls the Belgian 'Comité National' for feeding and clothing the people. He was so delighted to be visited by an English person desiring information and he entered into very full explanations of the American Relief Commission and the 'Comité National'.

It was evident that his relations with the Belgian 'Comité' were very good and sympathetic and he admired their organizing powers and their devotion. He was not so laudatory of the Americans who compose the Commission and it looked as if there had been friction. The tendency was to imply that they were businessmen *pur et simple* and were doing this work not only from philanthropy but from ulterior motives of eventually (even if they had not previously) establishing business connections. In this there may be some grains of truth, but undoubtedly it showed ignorance, real or feigned, of the great sacrifices and devotion of Mr Hoover and his colleagues. Especially Mr Hoover who I am told gave up a position bringing £50,000 a year to carry on the work of relief.

Many of the facts issuing from this talk are recorded in the Aide Mémoire. Captain Bruhn struck me as a singularly fine man. He has a sister in London married to an Englishman. A man of feeling too – but of course his best qualities a bit handicapped by the singular and anomalous position he was filling. He promised me to arrange that I should see the people fed. The following day he sent me a magnificent bouquet of crimson roses.

We returned to the hotel and lunched together still talking – my Baron told me much about the naval battle, which he evidently considered a Victory, but he said that when the first telegrams came he and von Moltke agreed not to believe it – it was incredible – too good. Then confirmation constantly followed and to their minds the greater tonnage destroyed on the British side decided the matter. Later on people disputed this and in England I find it also considered a victory. To my mind Death was the victor – *Death* and *Destruction*.

Then I went to rest and he to do an hour's work. My invalid ways and unusual hours for meals were an astonishment to him. At first

I fancy he was a bit suspicious of them, wondering if they were excuses for getting rid of him, but after a couple of days he understood. And in reality I was glad enough of his company for there were no letters to write or answer, no single book in the hotel and of course, except my phrase book, I had none and only two Belgian papers to read which had little in them. Three or four out of the ten days of my stay these French papers did not appear, being all confiscated.

Conditions: I had no paper to write upon except the notebook I had brought and that I was under orders to submit to the authorities before leaving Belgium. Often I wished to have a chat with the waiters or porters or chambermaid, but beyond the necessary exchange of words I never did, fearing they might be spies placed there to inform if I contravened the rules.

It was cold, wet and very windy and I found it hard to walk against such odds – I could not have done so if it had not been for the relief of descent from the altitude of Berne. We walked again rather forlornly about Brussels and arranged to visit Antwerp the next day. I forgot to say that the Baron took me that afternoon to a smart restaurant for tea. I did not want to go, it being discordant to my feelings to be seen eating in a public place with a German officer and an unpleasant sense of being stared at by men who were evidently Americans made me determine not to go again. I suppose he noticed it as he never suggested it again. I only took a cup of chocolate which cost 1fr.

Saturday, June 10th The morning promised better and we trammed to the station. A good deal of this Central Station is shut up and at the turnstiles passports and passes have to be shown as well as tickets. Soldiers standing sentry everywhere. As the Baron did everything for me I had of course no trouble, but I knew by old experience what a nuisance it must be to the population. Yet a goodly number of people always seemed to be travelling. I noticed that the Railway Stalls were covered with German papers and books. I won't say to the exclusion of all other, but vastly preponderant. We agreed to my joy to take 2nd class for all our trips. I had not liked to ask fearing there might be some objection and I was relieved when he proposed it. This first journey was exciting. I wanted so much to see Malines [Mechelen] and bombarded Antwerp. There was not however very much to see en route. The tower of Malines, beautiful as ever, was the chief feature of our little trip and there was a bridge that had been blown up by the Belgians and rebuilt by the Germans and there was this tiny village of Duffel where some houses had been ruined and a certain amount of damage done to the Church. But the landscape as a whole was green, fruitful and smiling – there was little to make me think of a devastated country. I was very much astonished. There did not appear to be any systematic destruction though I have since heard there was at Visé and Tirlement.

We ran into **Antwerp**, and looking hard to find them I saw a house here and there ruined in the outskirts of the town and a few with just windows broken. Outside the Main Station up the long street and to right and left there was not a sign of destruction of any kind. I determined to walk in order to search more at leisure for any signs of war and we went up the long street and past the Royal Palace finding everything in statu quo. The sun was bright but the clouds were magnificent and boded ill. It was extremely cold. Then we reached the Shoe-market and there found a small block of houses completely ruined. It is supposed they were aiming at some Municipal buildings which are nearby. The Groenplatz was untouched and we crossed it to gain the Cathedral and see how it had fared. It was unimpaired. We went outside and scrutinized the façade well having heard that there was one mark somewhere, but it was not visible to the lay naked eye. We walked about a good deal on all sides seeking the ruin one expects in a bombarded town, but we could find none other. Then alas! thunder began and a deluge of rain so we sought a restaurant for shelter and luncheon. There seemed to be only one which my Baron was willing to enter; he absolutely refused to go to all others though we passed several – it was evident to me that he feared to meet the population. The one we visited was quiet, good and not dear. Surprising how even in the midst of war, Continental restaurants manage to produce a better-cooked and more savory meal at a lower price than one can get in London.

The rain had been a deluge and while my Baron looked for the restaurant I had to shelter in shops. It was extraordinarily tempting at such moments to talk to the people and learn their points of view but I felt my parole would not permit of that. After lunch it cleared, though a terrific and icy north wind prevailed, nevertheless we went to see the old buildings in that wonderful Square near the docks, not a stone was touched – everything safe – and on to the docks which more than anything else showed the effects of war in Antwerp – I had last seen them full of shipping, active and busy, now the docks were a deserted wilderness – only the grass growing thick over the rusty truck rails.

When too cold and exhausted to walk more I took the tram and thus saw more of the town – the trams in all the large towns are running and manned by Belgians as usual. We got some coffee to warm us at the station in a large barrack-like waiting room evidently given up to soldiers, and the sun coming out I got a little warmed by the time we reached **Malines**. Here we spent a long and interesting afternoon. It is only about 25 minutes from Antwerp. The glass roof of the station was riddled with holes and in the station square, two or three houses have their windows broken and are boarded up or covered with sacking. Taking the tram up the long main street to the Cathedral we could see that a number of the houses had broken windows and curiously enough none of them seemed repaired though many (not all) of them were still inhabited. This may have been scarcity of glass or of labour or absence of the owners or of money – or still more likely a desire which seemed evident in the towns to leave things as they were. Malines had been fought over by the two sides – and shewed signs of this. We visited the Cathedral at once; the Baron pointing out to me with considerable fairness which bombs must have come from the Belgian and which from their guns. It seemed to me that the worst harm had been wrought by the concussion – which had shattered the priceless windows and bits of jewelled glass lay about the ground. The gable and buttress at the west end can be repaired, but the glass never can be restored. So sad to see and so wonderful to think it could have escaped with so little structural damage, little at least so far as the eye of the amateur could judge. The fine old tower shewed no injury. Service was held in part of the church (I believe this statement to be accurate but I must verify it from my notebook left in Berne). I stooped and picked up many bits of the coloured glass lying in the débris and some street children seeing me do this followed suit and soon began to follow me down the street bringing bits for sale. The officer looked askance at all this – not forbidding but not officially approving and indeed remarked that he ought not to allow it. However he let it pass and I brought away these treasures, wondering how the inhabitants had let them lie there so long. I fancy I started a new industry in Malines that afternoon.

The Cathedral precincts seemed to me more marred than the Edifice itself – two or three rare old houses of a public character probably being destroyed all but the walls. Everywhere I marvelled why the flames which gutted such buildings failed to touch adjacent houses on either side, but it is a feature of the very limited nature of the destruction in Belgium that destroyed houses are often to be seen dotted here and there amongst others quite untouched. Not far from the Cathedral Square a block of houses was completely levelled and there, a few men were at work evidently with a view to begin reconstruction. The large Church where the Rubens formerly hung was untouched as far as one could see, only in this case also the lofty windows had suffered from concussion and the vacancies filled with plain glass. Services were going on and it was impossible to do more than ask the verger for news of the Rubens. He pointed to the Crimson Curtains behind which it had hung, and assured me it had been removed for safety. He was uncertain where, but believed it to be in London. As we wandered on we found streets adjacent to the main street which had suffered somewhat severely, while around the Station the houses with windows shattered, though numerous, were the exception rather than the rule. Altogether Malines has been marked with a mark that generations won't obliterate, but to have been the scene of conflict between two such forces and have escaped so lightly in modern warfare is a marvel.

There was a great crowd of civilians at the station for it was Whitsun Eve and the crowd of workmen and the gala appearance of the women suggested that they were going away for a week-end holiday. Outwardly, they were bright and happy. My Baron drew back and aside as much as possible in his habitual way. It was late when we got home, tho' the endless daylight made me wholly forget the hours. The officer told me that the Belgians had greatly resented the change of time, as a German innovation – but it was enforced and those who stuck to their old time simply found that, for instance, school was well advanced before their children arrived.

We agreed to visit Charleroi next day and he left me at the door of the hotel lift. We had supped in Malines at a little station restaurant.

Whit Sunday, June 11th This was a long day necessitating an early start. The day seemed drier. We took a tram to the station on the lower side of the town and just caught a less comfortable train, these being old Belgian rolling stock, ill-built and shaky. My Baron said the Belgians spent little on improving their railway carriages. We passed Waterloo and saw the pyramid marking the battlefield and surmounted quite safely by the metal lion, said to have been taken away by the 'Huns'. The train crawled and we could see the whole field very clearly and the farm Houanmont etc. It was curiously under the circes to have the points explained to me by a countryman of Blucher – now an 'Enemy'. Oh! the inconsistency and shifting policy of nations!

There was absolutely no destruction – that I could see, though I looked diligently for it – on both sides the line, in any of the villages or little towns that we passed in that three hours' trip. The country looked lovely, verdant and flowery and the country folk looked healthy and well-fed.

At last we reached **Charleroi** and a very ugly place it is, a coalmining straggling town with no fine buildings and no picturesque streets. It was Whit Sunday, cold and occasional showers. No cabs to be got. I found about twenty ruined houses in the street leading uphill to the left as you leave the station. Then one came to a street cutting across that along which the trams ran. We took it and in the Boulevard Rodin (I think it is called) found 2 or 300 yards where houses had been more or less wrecked. But some hours spent walking and tramming about the town revealed no more. All seemed just as ordinary. Here, as universally in Europe, children were selling false flowers for Red Cross or prisoners. At the very top of the town near the Industrial School for boys there is a 'Place' from the surrounding wall of which one can see the town and the mines and almost the entire district. No ruin was visible. I was told but of course I could not verify that nearly 90 per cent of the normal output of coal was being produced, but whether this was or was not being used by the Germans for themselves or was going through ordinary business channels I cannot say.

There was a great to-do in the big hall of the Industrial School for an Exhibition was being held of the hand-work they had done and it was being sold also I think for the Red Cross. Sorely against his will I made my Baron come in. It was very full and he evidently feared in his uniform some insult. However I noticed no discourtesy, only he was uneasy till he had dragged me out again. There was metal work, wood-carving, pottery and all the usual ugly and useless handicrafts. A girl made me buy two metal pin trays of beaten iron like ivy leaves – (and later on my arrival in London I gave one of these to Henri Lambert the glass manufacturer of Charleroi). There was a deal of refreshments and a band. The people looked very cheerful and gay. I noticed the things I bought together with all the others were tied up with Belgian colours – at least my Baron pointed it out to me, remarking that it was against rules and ought not to be allowed. Afterwards we walked through the park and wound by another road back to the Centre where, as it grew late, we got some supper and then walked about again until the train was due. At this time the people poured into the streets for their Sunday outing and they looked I must own happy and cheerful. Doubtless the other side was not to be seen. Obviously it is a well-to-do town. We searched along the banks of the River Sambre for rumoured destruction but were unable to find any.

It was late when we reached Brussels – twilight – that is to say about 10.30 p.m. To me the day had been fairly interesting but my poor Baron was obviously bored to death. And if I had but been allowed to talk to the people how very interesting it would have been.

We travelled with many officers – handsome and singularly serious looking men. I had expected the 'Junker', much abused man, to be very different and to be very repulsive to me personally – but on the contrary they were very calm cultivated serious dignified looking men, fully conscious of the awfulness of their destiny on the Western Front and of their work. I shall never forget one of them – a young dragoon, I called him Siegfried – and I have never certainly seen so perfect a human specimen. Naturally too, the grace and beauty of the dragoon's uniform, with its long pale blue cloak helped to increase the splendour of his appearance. Tall, slender, well-built, very fair with deep blue serious eyes that looked only at far away things – and perfectly moulded features he riveted my attention and I could not take my eyes off him. All German officers when they come into each other's company bow with dignity to each other when total strangers, and sometimes also introduce themselves by giving their surnames. Backwards and forwards officers were going daily from Berlin to Lille and Lille to Berlin, but mostly towards Lille. Four expresses every day were running from Lille to Berlin with restaurant cars and doing the journey in eighteen hours to the minute. The Germans are working breathlessly without pause or stay.

Whit Monday, June 12th Baron von [der] Lancken had returned from Berlin and in the early morning I was taken to see him (my notebook will shew, but I feel sure it was this Monday morning). He kindly came downstairs to see me and we talked in the beautiful Empire Reception room where earlier I had seen Count Harrach. He seemed tired and worried. I laid before him my great desire to go to Berlin and Ruhleben Camp, the more so that the unexpectedly strict character of the regulations binding me in Belgium had made my work of a very limited, almost useless character. He promised to do his best and to wire at once.

It was not until later that I learnt from my Baron that the military authorities in Belgium were not aware of my presence and obviously the Political Department felt nervous lest it should be discovered and not approved. Nevertheless they constantly referred to General v. Bissing as a 'very fine man'. Both in Belgium and Berlin I found wide divergence of opinion between the Military and Civil Departments. The 'War Office' always undoing the good and pacifying attempts of the Civil Departments. Baron von [der] Lancken was very pessimistic, he evidently felt very keenly the lying Campaign against Germany.

We started for **Louvain** – as usual in the rain, but when we got there it lifted a bit. We lunched in the train and so were prepared for a long afternoon. The Commandant of the town met us at the Station. Captain Kreuter (?notebook) a most charming and handsome young man of about 30. He wore a long and ample dark green cloak. We were introduced and he inquired what language he should speak running over a list for choice. I laughed and said 'English'. 'Ah! Then you are an American.' 'No', I said 'English'. He gave a start of surprise and bowed. I said 'It is a secret, please guard it'. 'With my life', he said gallantly and we walked off together. Outside he had a trap and horse ready for me. First however, he took me to the centre of the Station Square and described to me the events of the night of August 24 or 25. The Station Square is large and wide and all the houses that surround it are wrecked. They were chiefly small restaurant Inns. Louvain has two other large Squares, viz the Old Market and the Place de Peuples. The Germans assert that they had been in the town since the 19th, that the town was perfectly quiet and that notices had been affixed saying that if the people kept quiet nothing would happen to them, and that their men were bivouacked in the three Squares and their bayonets stacked.

Suddenly a rocket was fired in the early evening and at that signal the German soldiery were fired upon from the houses, roofs and cellars of these three Squares. In the Station Square the fighting was fierce, the soldiers retaliating upon their unseen foe and setting fire to the houses in order to get them out. The fighting continued up the Station Street nearly the whole of which is ruined, only walls remaining. In the Place de Peuples the attack was less severe for only a part of the houses are ruined and those are scattered in and out amongst other houses quite untouched. Moreover the adjacent streets are unimpaired. The affair in the Old Market was more serious for the end wall of the famous Library comes down to the Square. Beneath it in a *rez de chaussée*, are always kept the piled up heap of tents and canvas booths belonging to the market. The evening was dry with a light breeze and by reason of the fighting and firing these canvasses caught fire and burnt like timber. The Library above was soon in flames. German soldiers turned round with Belgian citizens to extinguish the flames and helped work the town pump. The Library was broken into, to find the fire extinguishers, but actually that valuable building contained none, nor was any custodian to be found. The books caught quickly and nothing could be done. The building is gutted and only the walls and gable remain today. The greater part of the Old Market is untouched only (as in the Place de Peuples) some of the houses are wrecked. Unfortunately as the flames streamed into the sky the wind blew the sparks across to the roof of the Cathedral which also caught. The German officer, Capt Manteuffel, ordered a few houses adjacent to be blown up with dynamite to prevent the fire spreading to the Hotel de Ville and that unique building stands unharmed and untouched. Manteuffel himself rescued the painting, one of great value which hung in the Cathedral of St Pierre and carrying it out had it placed in the Volksbank where it is to this day. The fire was got under control, only the roof and Carillon being burnt, and the heat melting the leaded panes the old glass fell down and was smashed. Already it is freshly roofed and the nave (still smelling of fire) boarded off while Service is held in the Choir and transepts. Here I watched with deepest emotion German soldiers and Belgian Citizens kneeling side by side at prayer. I gathered some relics of glass and molten lead.

All this and much else was told me by the young Commandant who had been trained in London in the School of Economics. Some day witnesses of the two sides will face each other and the truth be it what it may, will be established. Two things struck me – one, that the story coincided with the description of the event as given to Eleanor Hobhouse by a young fellow of 17, a violinist of Louvain; the second that the position of the destroyed houses etc. fitted in exactly with the facts as related.

But for a few hours there must have been a wild scene in that quiet little Cathedral town, that lovely August evening.

As we stood in the Station Square, the officer told me that all the civilians caught with arms actually in their hands (and the arms were many and various) were arrested and court-martialled then, I think, one in every three, twenty-seven in all, were marched to that very spot and shot – and there buried. He added that he had had the bodies exhumed and given a 'beautiful burial' elsewhere. He was very sympathetic that young man. Further he told me that Louvain was a town of 44,000 inhabitants and 38,000 were living quietly there today. Perhaps an eighth of the town was destroyed – but as we drove about it seemed to me that was a very large estimate. Other fine churches in the town and all the other University buildings were unharmed. The exaggeration has been great. Only on the further side of the station a small suburb called Kesseloo is ruined – for the Belgian army making a sortie from Antwerp met the invaders there and they fought.

It was not allowed to buy or take photographs, but Capt Kreuter very kindly gave me a book of views as some aid to my memory. Cathedrals seen daily get dreadfully mixed. The respectable working classes of Louvain are suffering from the cessation of business and must perforce receive food from the Comité National.

I was taken to see Baroness Emmingen [? spelling] a German lady who, with helpers, has come to Louvain to do good to the people. They supplement the relief of the Comité National, by providing paid occupation, giving medical and other relief and by training children and girls. This lady's house and dispensary was shown to me and she kindly gave me a cup of tea for we were perished with cold and damp. Herr Kreuter had driven me all round and about and up to a high point whence I could see the whole town spread out before me. Of the 6,000 who fled, a good number of them are men under arms. He told me that in the country districts the peasantry had for the most part repaired their houses – broken often only in parts and that to date 1,600 had been so repaired in the Arrondissement [District] for which he was responsible.

There was much I longed to ask this affable man, but my brain was sluggish with cold and fatigue and the horrid feeling of being inquisitive was most restraining. I realized more and more that the value of my visit to Belgium lay only in being eye witness of all the material things as they were, and to the fact that the German Civil Authorities were kindly and just and honest in their administration of this country. Later too, I found out the enfeeblement of the people and their diseased condition following upon mal-nutrition. It was obvious that their rule has to be strict, because they too are subject to the military authority and this is holding the country against its will. They have reason for some nervousness because they do not know what arms the Belgians may have hidden and should the Allies have success on the Western Front it is always on the cards that there might be a civilian rising and untold carnage (I heard nothing, of course, of the arrests and executions for treason which were and are of weekly occurrence). I do not think their martial law administration was any more strict than that under which I lived in South Africa – in the Free State.

I parted with real regret from Herr Kreuter (Parsifal I called him) a romantic figure, full of noble and ideal dreams and desires. It was in everything a day to be long remembered. He told me the Chilean Ambassador had been there and he told him that in asking for his Passport at the London Foreign Office he had mentioned his desire to see Louvain and the reply had been – There is nothing there to see, the town is completely destroyed!

It was late when we got back to Brussels and I went straight to bed to get warm.

Tuesday, June 13th This morning early we started for **Aerschot** having to go again to Louvain and change. Of all the cold days I think this was the coldest. We passed through a fresh bit of country but saw no devastation. When we reached the little station it was pouring rain and no vehicle to be got. We crossed the opening and took shelter in the little Railway Inn. Here we had a cup of coffee while Herr (name in notebook) who was sent with me to explain Aerschot (he being a member of the Commission that had taken evidence about the murder of the German Commander, Captain Steugel) went into the town to try and find some conveyance. My Baron evidently dared not go on account of his uniform, but Herr Xxx was in civil clothes and half a Belgian being a resident of Antwerp. He was very friendly, but I did not like him much – a man of totally different calibre to the others I had met – not a gentleman. Moreover, I did not think his information accurate nor that his facts tallied! He was one of the Germans long resident in Antwerp and intermarried with the Belgians.

At last he came back saying no vehicle was to be had in town and there was no help for it but to walk - which we did. First we met a company of German soldiers who at sight of an Officer did the 'Goose Step' which looked exceedingly funny. It appears to be the etiquette on meeting an officer if impedimenta prevent other forms of salute. The town is small, about 8,000 inhabitants and there seemed little destruction. We came at last to the church which we lionized. Outside no harm – inside none either – only one thing – the western door of the church had (I suppose) been struck by a shell and set on fire for it was burnt and the flame had bLanckened the wall just surrounding it and two out of three pictures hanging close by had been burnt, the charred frames still hung on their nails, the canvass hanging in tags. They were valueless as works of art, but no doubt interesting to the townsfolk – about 200 years old, a bad epoch judging from the bits left and the companion one remaining untouched. The heat had melted the lead of the window panes above the door and some of these had fallen out and had been renewed but there was no good glass here. The Germans affirm that if a shell hit this door it must have come from the Belgians, they being on the West. It seemed to me just as likely that it came from no shell, but the harm was slight and there is at present no evidence. The doorway is boarded up.

No other sign of war was to be seen in the picturesque winding streets of the little town till we reached the square where the famous outbreak took place and the Commander Capt. Steugel was found murdered on the floor of his room. We stood a long time in this Square, while Herr Xxx told the story of the affair as it was determined by the German Commission of Enquiry. This of course can be read in the German White Book on the Belgian Atrocities. We looked long at the Burgermeister's house, M. Tielmann, – a small corner house. The Balcony covering the two middle windows is shared by the two rooms. [See Plate 5]

The lad, a boy of 15, is supposed to have come out of his room onto the balcony in the dusk and seeing the Captain in the glare of the candlelight dressing for supper in his room, shot him through the open French windows. The shot was like a signal and immediately the soldiers in the Square below were attacked from the windows and roofs of the Square. Three or four houses in the Square are ruined or have broken windows. To my mind the weak point in this story is that there are two bullet holes in the first window (see black dots) which would indicate that he had been shot from the opposite house in the little Square. When I pointed this out to the Herr Xxx he was for a moment non-plussed, then said quickly that the original glass panes of the second window had been taken away for evidence before the Commission and new ones put in! Before that he had stated that the lad shot through the open window. The next day I got the book and pointed out to my Baron the inexactness of his statements and he, after a while, agreed with me. I did not like the man.

It was extraordinary how little destruction there was. We went to another part of the town and on the further side of the river there was an outlying part destroyed. Altogether it is said about a tenth part of the town. I saw a number of children coming out of school and these looked pretty well. A quaint little town. A tram was running. The rain began again and the wind was furious. We had to get back to the Inn, wet through and frozen. For the first time in my life I took a half glass of gin in boiling water and thereby I believe I saved myself from severe cold and lumbago. Then I begged to be allowed to dry myself by the kitchen fire which was conceded and the kindly womenfolk let me sit by the stove while they got us a meal. And such a good meal it was – for the men a big beefsteak, for us all a grand omelet of six eggs and delicious vegetables. I watched them cook it and they talked to me a little the while – asked me with curiosity if I was the Officer's mother? I did not dare ask much of what Aerschot had gone through, nor of present affairs. When our meal was over so was the storm. Our clothes were dried and we left by the afternoon train. At the Brussels station we fell in again with von Moltke and I was glad to take a cab to the Astoria. My Baron sat with me during my supper at which the sad-looking waiter officiated.

Still no definite answer from Berlin and the time was passing quickly.

Wednesday, June 14th This morning we confidently expected news from Berlin. My Baron was very anxious to go and forwarded my request in every way possible because he was so very anxious to see his young wife. He had told me of their meeting in the Alps and of their marriage immediately followed by the outbreak of war – so that in less than six weeks they were separated and except for a few days had not since met. He was evidently very anxious about her and deeply in love. She is an Austrian. They have two little children. But the reply had not come and so I wanted to go to Dinant. However the weather was so appalling, cold, wet and rough that after my experience at Aerschot I was really afraid. I regret now that I did not persevere, but indeed I felt very ill.

We fixed to see a Communal Kitchen. Captain Bruhn's Department had arranged this for me, and I had asked to see one in the poorer part of town. A member of his office was sent with me, a gentleman in plain clothes, somewhat Jewish looking and rather stupid. My Baron told me he was the brother of the richest man in Germany! He did not speak English well – but it was deemed unwise for an officer in uniform to go to these kitchens!!! So he was sent and I was rather glad as it gave me more opportunity of talking to the Belgian Manager of the Depôt. This was the only real and open conversation I had with a Belgian during my ten day's stay and though short, in French, and amongst a crowd of people and I had to stand which always makes me empty-headed yet I managed to learn a good deal. I have described in my article the general aspect of the queues – the people neat and trim (not ragged) quiet and orderly and subdued – but with worn faces and blue shades under their eyes – hungry looking and fragile, not ill like the Boer women – but getting ill. I asked him at once if there was any general enfeeblement of the people or increased mortality noticeable, and he told me of the serious outbreak of tuberculosis affecting largely the glands of the neck and filling the hospitals with patients, particularly adolescents, who stood in need of extra foods, very costly in these days. This disease was rapidly on the increase. The people received daily bread and soup and on stated days other things such as coffee, lard, sugar, rice, beans and a little money according to the numbers in the family.

The food looked good – but not sufficient. This Belgian Manager looked very good-humoured and smiling and willingly told me all I wished. Afterwards when I told my Baron about this tuberculosis he seemed seriously disturbed and even annoyed and it was plain that I was not being allowed to know the truth. We lingered by the fish market where the people were buying mussels, much loved of Belgians. We bowed off the dull Herr Xxx and tried to find Capt.

Bruhn to ask him details on this point – but he was not in. The Baron urged me to do some sight seeing but I was loath.

After lunch and rest he came to take me to the lower part of the town to see the factory for women and girls, set going by the Germans, partly no doubt to provide them with work and partly to get all kind of bags and sacks made. It has been said to me that these sacks were for use in the trenches but I can only record that I did not see any of that kind in the Factory nor amongst the great rolls of material anything suitable. 750 women and girls were at work and a more cheerful set I have rarely seen. Many were of a type far above that class of work. They worked great sewing machines propelled by electricity. They were paid three francs for a day and their dinner and a cup of tea or cocoa (I think). Some in higher positions got up to five francs a day. The material and machines were supplied by Germany. A German matron superintended the adjacent kitchen and the distribution of food, and a German Red Cross Nurse had a wee dispensary where she tended cuts, bruises and other ills, a singularly pleasant woman taking real deep interest in the characters of the young women in her care. There was also a crèche where married women brought infants, and I saw fifty babies there and two large airy rooms with baths and cots and every nursery necessity and nurses.

I did not take to the woman in charge of the Kitchen (a handsome and well educated person). She was inquisitive too and curious as to who I could be.

Coming back from this interesting experiment I got out near the station to buy white paper for packing not having dared bring a morsel with me. The Baron did not like my doing even this bit of shopping – but I did it.

Thursday, June 15th I was set on going to **Dinant** but the weather was really terrific, the worst day we had had. My lumbago threatened, I was sick with cold and feared to be laid up in bed. I dared not run that risk. We decided not to go, but later when the clouds lifted he took me out and I insisted on being taken to a shop to get a warm long sleeve vest. With difficulty I found something – evidently the choice of warm woolens was not large and as soon as I got home and put it on I felt my pains relieved.

Then we found Capt. Bruhn and had a talk with him about the tubercular trouble. I was glad to find he was aware of it and though perhaps he tried to make light of it, he owned that it was being enquired into by an American Doctor on the Commission. (This has since been issued as a Report by Dr. Lucas and is very important.) He laid stress on the impossibility of coping with this trouble owing to the blockade. The people are caught in a vice. Their patience is marvellous.

Leaving him we turned in to the Picture Gallery which I was anxious to see in order to know if any had been removed. My Baron said it was the French and Napoleon who did that sort of thing, and I felt guiltily that so also had we in South Africa. Kitchener brought away Kruger trophies from Pretoria and Lord Roberts Mr Fischer's Silver-Wedding Silver Tea Service etc and officers and men took every sort of thing which I saw in their kits from sewing machines and silver candlesticks to old Bibles.

Brussels gallery anyhow is untouched. Stocked as thick as the walls can hold with beautiful works of art. Climbing the long stairs had made it impossible for me to enjoy them.

After lunch the Baron said he was so busy at the office that he wanted me to come and sit in the Reading Room of the Political Department and read English newspapers. Having nothing whatever to read or write I was thankful for the suggestion and to my astonishment I found there *The Times, Morning Post,* and *Manchester Guardian* of June 13. I asked with surprise how these could be so quickly in Brussels – and at first my Baron was going to tell me, but suddenly recollected he must not and said nothing. I said it seemed impossible that they could come in that time from Holland – and from his manner I judge they come in some other way. However, I sat there and read for a couple of hours, glad enough of the news, but dreadfully depressed by the English attitude too apparent and absolutely contrary to Peace ideas. It was particularly distressing to read our Press there in the midst of the enemy and see it with their eyes.

A German civilian came in and sat down beside me to read. An oldish man, who spoke politely telling me he had lived much in England and how he bewailed this war and what a disastrous mistake it was. The same story everywhere – whenever I have met Germans all felt and feel that war with England was contrary to their wishes and against their every feeling – and never should have been.

We wandered out and the sun getting the upper hand for a bit, we went down the long hill to the beautiful and historic Square. On my way I bought chamois leather to cover my back and arm. In the Square with its gilded architecture not a stone was touched – indeed, Brussels is without a scratch.

That ended my day and I resolved if the Berlin reply did not come, to go to Dinant on the following day.

Friday, June 16th Again, the most awful weather. Cold intense, but more bearable with my woolen vest and chamois leather gird-ings. Dinant impossible – it would have been madness - and worst of all no word from Berlin. I felt in despair, for I had been so restricted in Belgium that my trip would have availed little if I did not get to Berlin. However, my faith in it would not give way for from the outset of the war I had always intuitively felt that one day I should go both to Belgium and Berlin and speak face to face with the members of the government.

We waited a lucid moment to walk first to the Political Department then to Capt. Bruhn's who was out – and now and again passing those mournful queues standing in the bitter cold and wet. At last I gave in and promised to do as my Baron wished, viz visit the wonderful antediluvian animals in the Natural History Museum about which he raved. I hated spending a modicum of my slender strength on such things at this moment. About 3 p.m. we went; it was a very long way in the tram and then a stiffish walk uphill through the park, but certainly the skeletons were wonderful and I am glad to have seen them, tired though I was. They are found not far from Charleroi. My Baron was much excited over them. We saw quite another part of the town and found everything *in statu quo*. He supped with me that evening and we were both depressed.

8

EMILY'S JOURNAL: BERLIN

To me Emily's visit to Berlin is extraordinary. We see her as she really is – a very remarkable and unusual woman.

One has only to look at her achievement. She arrives in Berlin on a Sunday morning. She knows little of the language. She has one address, that of Elisabeth Rotten who took care of the welfare of the internees. That address turned out to be wrong, and yet in five days she manages to see the chief people to do with social welfare and feeding; she sees the Foreign Secretary and discerns that he is willing to talk peace, and produces a plan of how such talks could begin without loss of face, to which he agrees (but does not wish the British to know he has agreed); she visits the camp for civilian internees and produces a plan for their release – or internment in a neutral country if of military age; she meets with leading and influential pacifists – which the political department specifically did not want her to do; in politics, she meets a leading socialist and also meets a leading pastor; and she manages to keep her German 'captors' happy, and she is meant to be an invalid. She leaves Berlin on the Thursday evening.

Although one could consider Emily to be lenient towards the foe, this is not a 'mischievous old woman' as the Foreign Office or Scotland Yard would like to call her, nor a traitor. This is a highly intelligent, well-organised woman, who knows what she wants. Her attitude has changed.

She sees the young men going to the Front and she knows there is a lot of heartbreak to come.

The Journal continues, still in Brussels:[1]

[Saturday, June 17th] I had expected him early [her escort, Baron Falkenhausen] but he tarried and I was getting anxious when suddenly towards 10.30 a.m. he appeared with radiant face to say the answer had come and we were to go [to Berlin]. We must leave at 3 p.m. that day. I said half an hour would pack my little box but I must get some food for the journey. So out we went, shopping as usual making him cross and we bought wine, eggs (39 centimes), cheese, butter, chocolate biscuits – none of it so dear as I had thought and I hastened home to lunch, pack and prepare while he went to get our passports all in good order.

At 2.30 p.m. he appeared, my bill was paid, and I was ready for him and we walked down to the station. It was the eve of [the anniversary of] the Battle of Waterloo, the wind had subsided and all looked very fair as we left. He was radiant and we both had the sense of being children let out of school. We took 1st class tickets and got a 'ladies' carriage and no one disturbed us all the way to Berlin. I looked my last on Louvain as we passed it and on Liège and the village of Doulain and the ruined house on the crag and then we ran into Herbestal and lo! Belgium with her many woes was left behind us. One felt so free in Germany by comparison. The Customs gave us no trouble and soon we glided on to Aachen. The spires were pretty against the evening sky – but I noticed that both there and everywhere else the factory chimneys were idle. I realized the blockade. I thought of Charlemagne buried there and wished I could have visited his grave as my ancestor. This I said out loud to the Baron who was a bit struck all of a heap that I claimed such Imperial descent – and immediately began to tell me that his family was descended from Hohenzollerns though it turned out to be a side branch and by a morganatic marriage …

He often chatted of his family and his visits to England, his friend there, Lord Wodehouse, and the Quickes in particular and the cruel blow of the war which had destroyed all his ideals. As we sped on, he pointed out the crops, green and flourishing – and at last about 10.30 p.m. as dark was falling, we rushed into the vast crowd of soldiers that filled Cologne station. It was packed. The Baron wanted to divert my attention from this sight (I had already seen it twice) and tried to drop hints about it and that Cologne always was full of men in this way. I said nothing, but of course I knew well enough the troops were massing for the Western Front and already twice before I had seen Cologne station thus packed with soldiers. Night fell as we left the station and hearing we were to have coffee at Magdeburg settled in for the night – a short night. The grey dawn saw me sitting up to watch the great northern plains of Prussia and to look at her silent factories and her well-cultivated fields. They were waving with the green corn looking on the whole in very fair condition. Then came Magdeburg and some very fair coffee and not dear. Everywhere cleanliness and order and every individual busy. Cheerful faces and many smiles, but no noise or laughter – a certain calm confidence. Then we flew past Potsdam – all so well arranged and ordered and uninteresting and then in no time we were in Berlin.

My Baron was all on the *qui vive*. He stretched his head out of the window very far, and I looked the other way. He cried: 'There she is' and rushed out of the carriage where I discreetly remained. However, they weren't a bit shy and soon began it again, quite like a couple of English or any other nationality. He introduced me and I found a very sweet girl with lovely eyes and a soft voice and quite delicious English. I felt friends with her at once.

He had decided to put me into the Fürstenhof but he and his wife were going to another Hotel which they always patronized and apparently he did not think it necessary to be always with me. I was thankful. It was only about 8 a.m. and I was glad to get a comfortable room and a good supplementary breakfast.

The Hotel was very comfortable and rather smart. My room was 10 marks a day (ruinous for me) but it had a private telephone to all Berlin and the book and hot water tap and self-emptying basin, and every convenience – and a balcony. My breakfast was excellent coffee, sufficient hot milk, two small pieces of war bread, one small roll, one pat of butter like a fat half crown and a good portion of excellent jam, and a little sugar. Brought to the room, this only cost M.1.50. The bread I never could finish and kept half for tea; the sugar I never take so the waiter asked leave not to bring it next morning. It was exquisitely served. (At the Westminster Palace Hotel for the same breakfast, but not served in my room and the items of poor quality instead of first class, and roughly served instead of delicately, I pay 2s.) The Hotel staff was almost entirely young men of military age – one could have raised a small company in that house alone.

We separated for rest and refreshment and at 10 a.m. back came my Baron to take me to the Kommandatur and I had my first drive through Berlin. I saw the Reichstag and turned under the archway into Unter der [den] Linden – a street of great disappointment to me for I had dreamed of an avenue of old and beautiful limes – with gnarled massy trunks such as used to form the avenue in front of St James Palace leading to Buckingham Palace and lo! there were only small inferior young trees mostly in cages still, like the newest street of a newly built suburb! It's a short street and has many restaurants and he pointed out the Embassies and the Royal Palace and so on and we got down at the Kommandatur. This gentleman is the Civil head, I believe, of the Berlin City Military body. I don't know exactly what it's called. He heard very sympathetically my reasons for visiting Berlin, noted that I wished to see Ruhleben, stamped my passport to frank me and assured me I need not then report myself daily to the Police. He wished all success to my work and said a few words in regard to his sorrow that England was fighting them. He shook hands very warmly.

We walked away – I was half in a dream and half dead with fatigue. We walked down Unter der [den] Linden to a restaurant where the Baroness was to meet us. I wished, as one means of studying the food position, to sample public places of every class. We began in a choice place where the 'best' people dined. It was very good and everyone seemed cheerful, especially the manager who was ubiquitous and most obliging. Here, to my surprise, we met Count Harrach, who it then transpired had also come to Berlin and was also staying at my hotel. I do not think however that he was there to exercise the least surveillance over me – I did not see him again till casually the day I was leaving.

I had an excellent omelet containing chicken livers – beautifully made and I think a green vegetable – and some fruit. I remember thinking it very cheap. My companions I noticed began with small lobsters or crayfish perhaps of which great quantities seem eaten in Berlin. But I believe they went on to meat, only as I came away, I do not feel sure. I felt a great desire to get away and be alone and to feel freedom once more, so I boldly excused myself, assuring the party that I could find my way home alone. They were a bit unwilling but

I shewed myself determined, feeling that I was now under no parole and as free as any other Englishwoman, even more so. I think 'twas a bit difficult for the two officers fresh from Belgium strictness to shake off that attitude of mind. Nevertheless, the fact that they wanted to be alone and enjoy themselves helped.

So I shook them off and found myself bowed into the street by the polite Manager – free the first time for twelve days. I thought I would stroll home, rest a while and then try and find Elisabeth Rotten.*

It was wonderful feeling myself alone in Berlin – in the very heart of the Country with which we were at war. I found my way back easily to the hotel and rested an hour with great comfort. Then I tried to find a cab to take me to Dr. Rotten's office in Friedenstrasse. All in vain – the few taxis were engaged, the still fewer horse cabs loathe to take so long a drive – one at last was willing but at such a charge I hesitated. Then it occurred to me to try and telephone to her. There was a 'phone in my room but alas! that first day I found it very difficult to understand or be understood through a telephone – I failed.

Suddenly I conceived the idea of writing to Herr von Jagow direct to announce to him my arrival in Berlin, to thank him for the permission afforded – to say how much I could have wished to thank him in person, desiring to do all that any one individual could do to bring our two Countries to a better understanding. I posted this and early the following morning by Express received a warm welcome to see him that evening.

I went out after writing and wandered a little about the town watching the people and wondering what link I could find. Then I took supper at the hotel and I think the Baron and his wife looked in to say Goodnight and told me my visit to Ruhleben was fixed for Wednesday [probably Tuesday as it was later postponed] and that he would call for me at midday on Monday to take me to luncheon. I went to bed with the sun streaming across me, glad of a long night

---

* Dr Elisabeth Rotten was born near Berlin to Swiss parents. By 1913 she was a lecturer at Cambridge University on German literature. She returned to Berlin in 1914 to help foreigners in Germany and co-founded the Bund Neues Vaterland and later the German League for Human Rights. She attended the 1915 International Women's Congress in The Hague, and worked for the foundation of the International Women's League for Peace and Freedom in Germany. She was instrumental in providing considerable help for civilian internees in Germany. Later, she became a member of the Society of Friends.

and anxiously wondering how to make the most of my visit and find links. How else could I study the Food Question and its effects on women and children? How I cursed my ignorance of German.

I found afterwards that Elisabeth Rotten had changed her address – hence the difficulty of telephoning.

Monday, June 19th I rose early much refreshed and determined to make the fullest use of my day. The Baron had agreed to call at 10 o'clock but to my relief rang me up to suggest noon instead – so I was free and went out. I secured a taxi and drove to Friedenstrasse. There I found Dr. Rotten had moved her office to Montbijou Platz and I drove there, keeping the taxi all the morning as they are scarce. It cost 12 marks. There I mounted a long flight of stairs and found myself in the office of the German twin to our Emergency Committee. I fell on them like a bombshell, this group of young women – fallen from the skies. We fell on each other's necks with joy. To me it was like native air to be with them and to know I could speak as I felt. Unfortunately, it was a frightfully busy week for them for they were arranging the meeting in Prince Lichnowsky's* house which took place the Wednesday. They understood at once all I wanted to do and to see and to know and at once suggested 'phoning Dr. Alice Salomon** for leave to see her Arbeiterinnenheim.*** Frl. Bölle took me, a very sweet girl who had become a keen Internationalist, and the taxi whisked us away. I was to see the needy working women at dinner – so first I had to telephone to my Baron to say I could not be back at my hotel at noon but would come later. It was delicious to hear what a turmoil he was in, anxiously questioning where I was and what I was doing, etc., etc. I replied I could not explain well through the 'phone – but I was doing the work I came to do. He was perturbed and, I felt, desired to limit my freedom. Later I learned from him that the War Office had given him orders that I was not to see anyone – but I held to it that I was not under parole as in Belgium and it would defeat the object of my visit. For what could I do in England if I told them I had only seen Soldiers and Officials? I stuck to it that I must see folk representative of every section, etc. He agreed to this in private capacity but

---

* Lichnowsky was German Ambassador to Great Britain before the war.
** Alice Salomon was a PhD and leading light in social work and schools in Germany. Born to Jewish parents, she converted to Protestantism in 1914.
*** Working women's home.

evidently his military duty perturbed his conscience. I made up my mind to say nothing but to go my own way. (But this is forestalling.)

Frl Bölle chatted to me as we drove along, pointing out the queues of impatient women standing outside the meat shops – and giving me details of the conditions relating to food. We saw the bedrooms, the kitchens, the dining rooms, and the people feeding or coming for food. It was close on 12 o'clock and they offered me my luncheon there. I accepted and had an excellent dish of potatoes, vegetables and thick gravy – the meat, of course, I did not take as I never do. Bread too. The whole meal was 30 pfennings – 3d – and tasty and well-cooked. Those who could not afford it had tickets from the Municipality. The matron was very friendly. I fancy they thought me an American. I dropped the Fräulein where she wished to go – a sweet girl – I hope we may meet again – and drove back to the hotel.

There I found von Jagow's letter welcoming me at 6 o'clock and there shortly appeared my poor Baron rather huffy to enquire what I had been doing. Fortunately, his sweet young wife was with him so not much was said. They were going to lunch to meet Herr Rieth of the Foreign Office who wished to meet me and were a bit upset that I had lunched. I explained that that did not matter, I could go with them and take a cup of coffee and see another class of restaurant and be introduced to Herr Rieth. The day was gusty and there were showers.

I then told the Baron that I had written to von Jagow and that I was to see him in the evening – whereat he at once said he must accompany me. We then all went together to the restaurant in the Leipziger Strasse where Herr Rieth met us. I took coffee only, good and moderate in price – and I noticed again that they eat lobster. Herr Rieth was very chatty and friendly, but all the same I did not take to him. He was to make the arrangements for the visit to Ruhleben.

As soon as possible I excused myself on the ground of fatigue, desiring to rest and be fresh for my interview with the Minister. I walked home alone – it not being far and past some of the smart Berlin shops all full of beautiful things and apparently busy.

I had rested about an hour when, to my great pleasure, Dr. Alice Salomon called and sat an hour talking in my room. While she was there my Baron called me up on the telephone attached to the wall and before I could prevent her, Dr. Salomon had rushed to reply. Of course there was confusion and I had to go and heard the Baron in his sternest tones demanding who was in my room speaking German. I told him, but he knew too little of the Social World [work] of Berlin to have any idea of Dr. Salomon, her work, or her international reputation. It took a long while to make him understand that she was the lady who had initiated the institution I had seen that morning and who, having been applied to for permission to see it, had heard I was here and naturally wished to call on me.

This explained, my interrupted conversation with Dr. Salomon was resumed. She gave me her views of the Food and Health situation in Germany and also Austria whence she had recently returned and I begged her to arrange for me interviews with leading men – a doctor, a clergyman, politicians, etc. She took an optimistic view of the public health, thinking indeed that with regard to infants and mothers it was even better than normal because owing to the scarcity of bread, philanthropic and municipal bodies were feeding the poorer classes with food of a more varied kind. She spoke much of the Aberdeens* whose intimate friend she is – and was very warm about my former work and full of gratitude for the effort I had made in coming to visit them during the war. She left and I made ready to go to Wilhelmstrasse.

The Baron came, rather stiff, and I repeated my assurances and explanation about Dr. Salomon. I wondered about it all, for I had been put under no restrictions whatever, the Kommandatur as he knew, had made me free and I was not on parole. I shewed him I could not study the Food Supply in Germany by sitting alone in my bedroom and I must see everyone I could and representatives of different classes. He was silent and only half convinced. I felt he had imbibed the Martial Law ideas of Belgium and brought them with him.

There was a flight of stairs at the Wilhelmstrasse and at the top stood the rather ubiquitous Herr Rieth. A curious, unpretentious, rambling old building – with long very narrow passages like old-fashioned Inns. I was shown into a waiting room where several gentlemen were awaiting interviews, but had not time to seat myself before I was summoned to the presence of the Minister and in another moment was ushered into a long room where von Jagow rose from his desk and came forward to greet me.

---

* Lady Aberdeen was President of the International Council of Women 1893–1936. Her husband was Lord Lieutenant of Ireland and then Governor General of Canada. By 1914 they were living in Ireland.

The room was very still and the windows gave upon a garden. He drew me to the window and placed me on a sofa with my back to the light while he sat on a low easy chair hardby [sic]. He was very simple and natural and wholly unofficial in manner.

I will not here reproduce our talk. I have written it out at length in a separate form and shall keep it apart and perhaps sealed. It lasted nearly an hour. I felt lifted into some sphere aloof from our blood-stained World. That I should sit in the Foreign Office of Berlin ere the war ended, I had always felt – it had been a piece of second sight to me – and there I was and it all looked familiar and as if I had seen and known it all before. A strangely moving experience to be sitting with the Foreign Minister of the country with which we are at death grips and having a heart to heart talk with what I believe was mutual confidence and respect.

Only all through I was tortured by my feeling of utter mental incompetence – partly from an empty brain, the result of over fatigue and partly from the sense that I was not trained enough maybe in public matters and diplomacy to make the most of a chance so unusual and so striking. I had the right spirit, but body and mind lacked power and knowledge. He probably thought me a goose, but if so, he was good-natured enough not to show it. When I rose to go I felt giddy and could hardly find my way to the door. The effort to concentrate my whole feeble mental powers had been very much too great for me.

Outside, the Baron and Herr Rieth awaited me. I recovered myself a bit, enough to say tauntingly to the Baron that the Minister had said I was to see anyone I pleased and the more I saw the better satisfied he would be and that I had told him I had seen Dr. Salomon and hoped he did not mind. He had said he was delighted I had seen her.

The Baron there at seemed much relieved – as if a weight was off his conscience. So we returned to the hotel and I hoped to rest go early to bed and digest the talk I had just heard. It was a relief that the Baron said goodnight, asking me to ring him up in the morning.

I went to my room – when to my joy in a very few minutes after I had eaten my boiled egg for supper – Elisabeth Rotten appeared asking if I would receive also Baron de Neufville, the well-known pac-ifist of Frankfurt a/M, the friend of the Courtneys to whose daughter I had sent the wedding gift last summer from Amsterdam on behalf of

Kate Courtney. I was most pleased. It was then a little after 8 p.m. and they stayed till past 10 – and then we sent the gentleman away first, that he might slip away the more unobserved – he fully aware of the necessity for caution. He brought me a bouquet of magnificent roses which sweetened my room all the time I was in Berlin. How we talked – they telling me and I telling them.

I was glad to seek his advice about an idea that had already come into my head since I left von Jagow, born of the feeling that it ought to have been a British Statesman sitting chatting with him and not just me. He thought I could do no wrong by suggesting it in a little note and outlined the form. I was comforted and supported and determined to try. They told me much of the condition of the country – he said food affairs were very similar at Frankfurt a/M and like everyone else he said on that point Germany would never give in. He spoke of the Peace Gatherings they had had at his town and they told me much that was helpful of the state of internal politics – the position and difficulties of the Chancellor, the respect felt for him, the link between him and the Kaiser – the continued Jingoism of the Conservative Militarists and the immense growth of the Social Democrats whose Minority in Reichstag was a Majority in the country and likely to sweep the Empire at the conclusion of the war. I spoke of my wish to see Clergymen and Frau Minna Cauer and anyone else possible. Dr. Rotten was so sorry that the Meeting for her Fund to take place at Prince Lichnowsky's house should have been fixed for that very next day, for it was all on her hands; otherwise, she could have done so much more for me.

By 10.30 p.m. I was alone to chew the cud of a most exciting and wonderful day. It was still broad daylight as I went to bed.

Tuesday, June 20th Very early I was up, desiring to write to von Jagow without delay. I hurried through my coffee and expressed the letter. Then Baron Falkenhausen 'phoned to say the trip to Ruhleben was put off as of some difficulty about a car and that Count Schwerin himself desired to be there. This somewhat wasted the day. He said he would come round later and take me to a restaurant. Dr. Alice Salomon rang me up about arranging for Dr. Lewandowski[*] and Heine[**] to see

---

[*] Lewandowski was the Leading Medical Officer in schools.
[**] Wolfgang Heine was a member of the Social Democratic Party and long-time member of the Reichstag.

me. I told her and E. Rotten how much I depended on them as otherwise isolated.

At noon came my Baron and said he would take me, at my desire, to another class of restaurant. I found it rather a long walk – he said Herr Rieth wanted to meet me there again 'to make arrangements about Ruhleben'. Somehow, I disliked Rieth, though most attentive and gentlemanly, but I shall always believe he was a spy. Half through lunch, Rieth, having been told where we were by telephone, arrived and my Baron as suddenly departed giving me over to his charge. Lunch ended and, at very moderate cost, he proposed taking me to see the Tiergarten, and when I pleaded fatigue, he said his car was outside. I could say no more and he drove me about to see the sights – through the wooded park, past the various public buildings, by the famous statue of Hindenburg – barbaric but life-like colossal figure – and then to his very charming apartment, exquisitely furnished. Here he found a pile of the London Times for me and as the cold showers were incessant, I begged to be taken back to my hotel. This he did, promising to come next morning at 10 a.m. I felt relieved when he was gone. Then I rested and got some tea in the lounge. They only served cake with tea, two or three very small thin slices and no bread and butter. I think, occasionally, stale rusks.

Later on when I was in my bedroom Elisabeth Rotten appeared. I was rejoiced. She was arrayed in her best for she had just come from the Emergency Committee Meeting at Prince Lichnowsky's house, a meeting which had been a huge success. She wanted me to take the news to London, she writing it to Berne to Gertrude Woker and I translating and forwarding it thence. She wished it to be in the London Press. We had a long, long talk – she said Baron de Neufville had much wished to come again but thought it wiser not to do so. She was very exhausted and several times nearly fainted. I gave her ether for her face and some brandy and had up some coffee for her. She said she had not had a single day off, not even a Sunday, since the war began. She told me much of her work and of all the men told her who came out of Ruhleben on parole to visit their wives – how, even, they were talking of bringing out from there superfluous food parcels for their wives and families in Berlin. She looked after their families. We talked long and deep of everything in both countries – of politics and prospects. She promised to send Pastor Siegmund-Schultze* to see me. Many she wanted me to see were away – many full up with work. She was trying to find time also for Minna Cauer** who wanted to see me. It was late when she left and I went to bed.

Wednesday, June 21st Very early I was up and breakfasted and had the room in order to receive Dr. Lewandowski at 8 a.m. He came with German punctuality – in full uniform and cloak and sword – with a nice honest face. He spoke English with difficulty but fair correctness. He spoke of the children of the town – was chief doctor of the Municipal Schools. He said there was undoubted enfeeblement among the infants under 1 year and the children from 10–14. He had however weighed all last year and again this year and found them normal. He knew of no increased mortality in consequence of this enfeeblement. This sounded strange to me. He went on to lay stress on the improved condition of mothers and infants owing to the food supplied them being more varied in character than what was customary in their lives. He could see no reason to think that the food shortage would necessitate 'giving in' as vanquished. He was very polite, and very grave but pleasant. All he said was in agreement with Dr. Alice Salomon but yet I did not feel I had got to the bottom of him.

Ruhleben

As soon as he left I began to prepare for the drive to Ruhleben. Very soon the car came with my Baron and Herr Rieth and soon we covered the 10 or 12 miles to Spandau. Rieth had brought lunch and we stopped inside the camp and ate sandwiches early though it was, for I saw a long and tiring day and no chance of food therein. Afterwards the gentlemen acknowledged my forethought.

I was taken first to the offices where I was received by Count Schwerin the German Commandant of the Camp. He was a handsome old man with a fine presence and a most benign countenance

---

* Schultze was the internationally known pastor and Chairman of the Juvenile Health Society of Berlin whose meeting with the English Quaker Henry Hodgkin just before war started led to the formation of the Fellowship of Reconciliation in England. He was imprisoned many times during the war.

** Minna Cauer attended the Women's Congress in The Hague. She kept a diary and said of her Berlin meeting with Emily: 'Interesting hours! Miss Hobhouse, English woman through and through, one woman of her race which one must admire and love …' The two women talked about German-British relations and felt that each country could offer something to the other.

– one loved him instinctively and from all, of both sides, one heard only good of him. He was really beloved and known to have done the best in his power to make Camp life endurable. He was full of the interest of it and spoke of the prisoners as 'meine grosse Familie'. Long and very boring explanations were given me in the office about the system employed and the autonomy granted – and at my request facts and figures about those who had left and those who were on the list desiring to leave. For many reasons large numbers of the elderly men did not wish to go back to England having their wives etc. and businesses in Germany. Those who did want to return were of military age and of course could not, unless invalids. At the moment only nine were applying for exchange. The monthly date for leaving was the 6th.

Then we went to inspect the camp and the old Count hearing I was weakly insisted, rather tryingly, upon offering me his arm, a thing so boring to us. However I was quickly introduced to Capt Powell the elected English Captain of the camp and his next in Command whose name I forget – I think Simmons. It was curiously stirring to be in a Camp again – with all its sordidness and all its artificiality, its neatness and its squalor, its dun colour and monotony, its forlorn efforts to find amusement and occupation, its shabbiness and the worn strained faces of the inmates.

Only in this camp there were no children, no raging sicknesses, no starvation, no skeletons, no deaths. The problem was different to that which had faced me sixteen years before in South Africa. All Camps are odious – that is the basis from which one must start in speaking of them. That odiousness is accentuated in the early days of formation because the inmates are brought together in a hurry with nothing ready for them – supplies, shelter or sanitation.

From that odiousness Ruhleben was not free, but given that, and all the suffering it involved, I can and must truthfully say that Ruhleben Camp was not a bad one – that much was done for the amusement and occupation and instruction of the inmates, that the food was good (the bread coarse but wholesome) and kindness shown by the Enemy authorities.

Nevertheless a cloud lay upon the Camp and as I walked about with the group of companions, often I was alone with Captain Powell and learnt from him of the mental and nervous strain becoming more marked, especially amongst the older men. I talked with several of these and found them in a strange condition. Capt Powell begged me to do all possible to get out the men of 45 and over, saying he just could not pull them through another winter and they infected the whole camp. Without them he felt the younger men could brace themselves to face it out. I promised to leave no stone unturned when I reached England to plead for their release. Moreover I spoke to many lads as well as old men and became more and more sure that the problem was mental and psychological not material. Some of the younger men also showed signs of great strain.

The civilian internees seem in every country less able to bear detention than do military prisoners of war and this for several reasons.

1st They feel Fate has been unfair to them.

2nd They have never been under discipline.

3rd They have not escaped from the more awful sufferings of war – the trenches etc.

4th They are usually older men and less adaptable.

5th The majority are married men and anxious about wives and families.

6th They are hurriedly taken from businesses without time to arrange - the future dark.

7th They have had no opportunity of having their fling – doing their bit – showing their loyalty.

8th Consequently try to shew loyalty to their country by the only means open to them viz putting themselves into a state of mental hostility to everything and everybody about them – even the food is 'hostile'.

9th To maintain this mental hostility at white heat is before long to become mentally deranged.

Dr Ella Scarlett Synge* has issued a good report of this Camp, so it is hardly necessary for me to dwell upon what I soon saw were the less pressing and important features of the life. I mean the kitchens, the food itself, the Canteen, the sleeping and living arrangements, Washing and Sanitation.

I thought the food good and excellently cooked and as much as the

---

* Dr Synge was a South African member of the Ladies Commission to investigate conditions in the camps in South Africa for women and children whose homes had been burnt by the British in the Anglo-Boer War of 1899–1902.

conditions in Germany made possible. Potatoes and fish that day and both were first rate. In a smaller kitchen men could, for 1d or 2d, have camp food fried or done up in some way and their own English parcel food also cooked for them.

The parcel delivery office was an immense business – dealing out some 1,250 parcels every morning. 39,000 parcels[**] had arrived during the month of my visit. In all the time the Camp had been running only two or three parcels had been missed out of this vast number streaming in.

There were many amusements golf, football, sports of various kinds – a great space for all this – Cinema, Theatre and Company perform-ing constantly, arts and crafts – an Exhibition of work proceeding – small gardens, poultry keeping – occupations of a more serious nature. Shops of many trades – two dentists, Police force of fifty strong. University attended by 250 with 9 or 10 professors, a library, hall, sepa-rate rooms for languages nicely furnished. YWCA hall, Protestant and Catholic Churches and a Restaurant nicely arranged where the older or more weakly might take their meals.

I thought in comparison with the many blessings of the Camp (as Camps go) that the sleeping accommodations came off worst though that was not bad as in the Boer Camps. I thought the men kept their barracks very dirty, and I told them so. Their excuse was 'no time'!!! Yet there were hundreds of merchant seamen there well accustomed to keep the deck of a ship spotless.

I saw the hospital for temporary illnesses and the doctor – a long and rather low building which did not look very inviting. There have, I am told, been only about six deaths in the camp and the health is good.

It was a long day. I seemed to be 'taking in' at every pore and felt much exhausted. At the end I asked leave to speak a few words to Capt Powell and his 'Aide' and I sat down and told them how much we felt for them and how none better than I knew the awfulness of Camp life. I told them of my experience of sixteen years ago – and of the awful camps we gave the Boer Women who with their children lay down and died without a murmur. I assured them that by comparison they were fortunate in Ruhleben, but that it was a hateful system and I would do my best in London to obtain release or exchange first for

---

[**] Many of these would have been food parcels sent from Berne.

over 45 – then for all. They must not think they would be forgotten etc etc.

I afterwards wrote a little letter to the Camp – on these lines and showing how they too, each one, held something of the honour of England in their hands to uphold or to mar as really any soldier in the trenches. This letter I sent to the Foreign Office open to be transmitted to Count Schwerin if he thought fit to communicate it to the Camp. I wrote it because the men seemed to me to need above all things a mental and spiritual tonic.

Large numbers of the men drew up to see us drive away; it gave a horrible pang to go away and leave them there – such a forlorn and despairing atmosphere hung about them. It was one of the most painful moments of my life and as such will always be remembered and the whole issue is stamped indelibly on my mind. The gates fell to and it was over. I was almost dead with exhaustion. I had been on my legs for hours – bad enough by itself and in addition going through tense mental work and strong emotion, having at the same time to be wary, offend none and keep outwardly calm.

And yet the mere physical control of my heart seemed to want all my limited powers.

Sanatorium at Charlottenburg

We drove to the Sanatorium in Charlottenburg where Dr. Weiler had his patients – those suffering mentally. There were about sixty patients at that moment – housed excellently in four or five well-furnished villas in a quiet avenue each in a pleasant garden. An Arab, a Jamaican negro etc, were amongst them. I spoke cheerful words to all. Dr. Weiler and an Assistant shewed me all. The treatment seemed excellent – in two classes – those paying for themselves and those paid for thro' the American Embassy. The former were in a really beautifully furnished villa, with single bedrooms like boudoirs. A group of men were here who made a very bad impression on me – real bounders – mostly suffering from heart trouble for which they had been going through a course at [Bad] Nauheim and there captured – their complaints were childish and ridiculous. I spoke very gently to them and explained matters, the doctor also spoke very gently. We did not forget they were heart patients. But they were unreasonable to an extent which showed they were also suffering mentally. Yet they were enjoying every comfort, even luxury, with the one great exception of their liberty and the need of obeying a few disciplinary rules such as lights out at 9 p.m. and no gambling for high stakes allowed.

I had far more pity for the men in the second class, who were two or three in a room (large airy pleasant rooms looking on the garden) for they were many of them in a sad condition bordering on insanity. I can't forget Mr Brakewell – an artist – or old David Lloyd (70) a seaman and others.

It is impossible in this short account to give any idea of the piled up information gained that long day by my own eyes and ears – apart entirely from the official side put before me, or the prisoners' side to some extent told me.

I shall always remember it as one of the fullest and intensist [sic] days of my life – during which every moment was lived by one's every faculty of mind and body to the fullest possible extent. And through all was the great drain upon one's sympathy.

We drove rapidly to the hotel. I was much exhausted – and thankful that the two men departed, appreciating my desire to rest. But I had not been long on my sofa before Elisabeth Rotten arrived bringing the dear old Frau Minna Cauer with her. We talked long and fully. Elisabeth Rotten confirmed that there could be no great need of food in Ruhleben as men allowed out on parole from there had proposed to her a plan for sending out parcels for a help for their families.

Frau Cauer was so sweet – she thanked me so earnestly for coming – she was deeply moved as she asked with tears streaming down her face: 'Dear, dear Miss Hobhouse – Why, tell me why, does all the world hate us so?' She went on: 'My people are honest, they are industrious and mind their own business and to me it seems without detracting from any other nation much less the English whom I have always admired – that my people are capable and clever and industrious. Why then are we hated?'

I could only say that I thought the dislike lay in that very fact – they were too capable and successful and the result was fear and jealousy from which hatred had grown.

They had been with me an hour when Dr. Alice Salomon came to take me to see Heine. It was a fine evening and we took an old open cab such as adorned the streets of Berlin at this moment and drove to a distant restaurant where it would be convenient for him to meet us. Dr. Alice asked me to come afterward and sup with her

– about 8.30 p.m. I had had no dinner, only those early sandwiches about 9.30 a.m. outside Ruhleben, and hardly a mouthful for tea and was faint with exhaustion. I felt I should not even hear what Heine said unless I were refreshed. So at the Restaurant while Dr. Alice went upstairs to look for him I asked for a cup of cocoa. I was vexed afterwards for I think she was surprised as if it reflected upon her hospitality and to my regret she insisted upon paying for it and adding biscuits. I was then able to hold out – but I noticed that she remarked several times that it would be a 'light' supper. Afterwards I understood more clearly why.

Heine came and impressed me very deeply, a grave weighty man. He spoke slowly and very clearly so that I understood nearly all he said and Dr. Salomon interpreted the rest. He is highly thought of in the Reichstag, a fine speaker – a leader of the Majority Socialists – who followed the government to war on account of the danger from Russia. He made me grasp as never before the way in which Germans regard Russia – it looms large in their eyes. He spoke chiefly, however, of the food question – and scouted the idea that it would oblige the government to make peace. He said people were suffering and would have to suffer privation – but that scarcity need never have been if the government had taken it in hand soon enough. He said that at the beginning of the Blockade the Social Democrats had drawn up a scheme of distribution and presented it to the Government. This (like all Governments) took no heed, and luxury and waste continued. Now point by point that scheme was being adopted. Meanwhile there had been a year's needless waste. He spoke of the 'great push' expected to begin in a few days. (It did begin in fact June 25th, two days later.)

It was a long interesting strangely moving conversation, as we three sat round the little table in the third-rate Restaurant – speaking in low earnest voices. At last he excused himself and bid us farewell and we went out to find a rare cab. With difficulty this was done – a strange old man to drive us and we reached Dr. Salomon's beautiful little flat. It was interesting this peep of a German 'professional' woman's flat. She had one maid and supper was ordered. While we talked, she told me much of her life, her work, her love for Lady Aberdeen (2nd mother to her) in whose house in Ireland she had been staying when the war broke out. She sent messages to Lady Aberdeen. At last supper was ready – and it certainly was light. In a moment I realised how short food was in private houses. There was an omelet made of one egg for the two of us, there were three very small and very thinly cut slices of bread – there was a very small dish of stewed cherries. In addition there was a small block of butter 3oz the total supply per head for two weeks. I realized I must only make a feint of taking any and just scraped it with my knife. As to the omelet we took tiny mouthfuls and eked them out with much conversation. She said they were content and were learning something fresh every day. Formerly they had cooked with so much butter and fat, now they adopted the English fashion of grilling their meat over the fire and found it enjoyable. She spoke much of the care Municipalities and Societies were taking of the poor and of expectant mothers.

It was still broad daylight when, after 10 p.m., the old cabman came again and she packed me in and told him to drive me home – which he did and I enjoyed the quiet drive in the late evening light. It was 11 p.m. when I reached the hotel after a very full day.

Thursday, June 22nd Up early. Falkenhausen 'phoned he would come round about midday and lunch with me. Rieth 'phoned from the Foreign Office for particulars about my English Passport. Baron von Ow also 'phoned from the FO to ask if he might come and see me at 11 a.m. Finally he came but rather late – a nice young man who had been in S. Africa at outbreak and got back from there to find himself under surveillance in London. Spoke of the great kindness he had received from Dr. Markel, whom he said I must see and thank - also the diamond king Ludwig Breitmeyer – messages also to many who had befriended him in England. While we were talking my Baron and his wife came and I had to introduce them. They were a bit stiff. Soon Count Harrach came also and we chatted awhile at length till we separated for luncheon.

I went with my Baron and Baroness to a Restaurant in the Leipziger Str. and excusing myself early walked back thro' the big shops. We were to meet at 6.30 p.m. to sup and get to the station when they two would part, poor turtle doves! I felt very sorry for them. She was very young and sweet and feeling it acutely. I did some shopping – or tried to – for my journey and went back to rest and prepare for my interview with Herr von Stumm, Head of the English Department at the Foreign Office.

I had not long been in before Elisabeth Rotten came and we talked much. She seemed very ill and exhausted. She told me Pastor Siegmund-Schultze was coming at 4 o/c. He was frantically busy. She offered to go and buy me eggs etc for my journey saying I could not get them because it needed a permit to buy eggs which I had not got. While she was gone the Pastor came. A tall fair man – loosely built – and singularly boyish-looking. He spoke English though not with ease. He told me details of the health conditions of women and children answering my questions as to the increase (if any) of mortality and the general enfeeblement of the population. After saying that the classes affected were children under one year and between 10 and 14 [years old] he gave figures saying that as Chairman of the Juvenile Health Society of Berlin all such figures came directly to him and I could quote him anywhere privately in substantiation of these facts. He stated that for the first twelve months of blockade or from the spring of 1915–16 one hundred more children per month died in Berlin – that the country districts were still normal – that the other great towns lumped together showed an increased total of 300 per month making a grand total of 400 a month or near 5,000 for the year. Of course to produce this increase a general enfeeblement was evident.

I asked why Dr. Lewandowski had failed to tell me this. He said because he was under military oath and unable to reveal such facts but he said 'it is nevertheless true'. Later on as he rose to go he said very gravely: 'We consider those 5,000 children to have been deliberately murdered by the British Government'. I said: 'Yes, I agree, but we consider that your Zeppelins and yr Submarines have murdered a large number of our children; it is murder on both sides'. He was a bit startled but agreed that it was so – and we shook hands solemnly. I liked him much. He spoke also of the lack of food, especially amongst his people in East Berlin where he lives and works. 'We are hungry, we are often very hungry; but we don't mind,' so he said.

When he was gone I walked to the Wilhelmstrasse and found awaiting me the ubiquitous Herr Reith. He quickly shewed me in to the office of Herr von Stumm – to whom I spoke much of Ruhleben. He told me the past history of the negotiations, and how anxious they were for total exchange – had indeed proposed it themselves twelve months before and been refused. But it must be all for all. They could not leave some there without hostages so to say on their side.

1. Emily Hobhouse 1912. Pencil drawing by William Arnold Forster, Fiesole, Italy. Emily said she was very ill at the time.

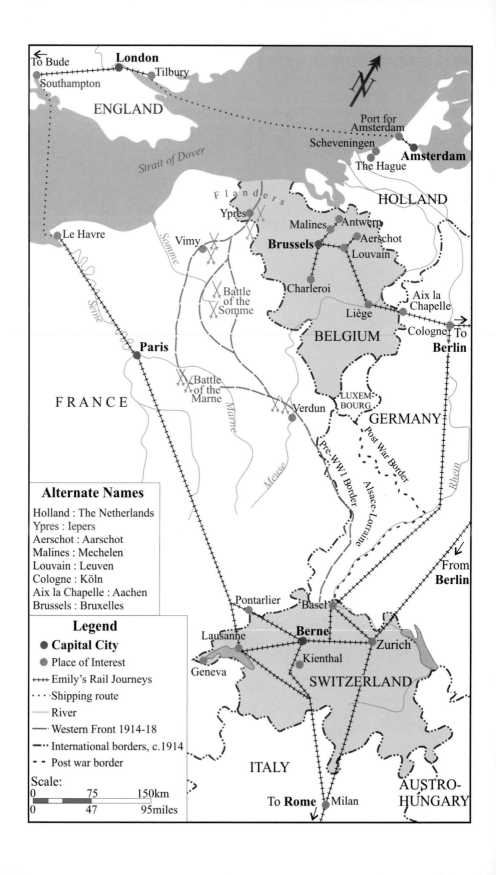

To Bude
London
Tilbury
Southampton
ENGLAND

Strait of Dover

Port for
Amsterdam
Scheveningen
The Hague
Amsterdam
HOLLAND

F l a n d e r s
Ypres
Vimy
Malines
Antwerp
Brussels
Aerschot
Louvain
Le Havre
Charleroi
Aix la
Chapelle
Battle
of the
Somme
Liège
Cologne To
BELGIUM
Berlin

Seine
Paris
Battle
of the
Marne
Verdun
LUXEM-
BOURG
GERMANY
FRANCE
Marne
Meuse

Post War Border

Pre-WW1 Border

Alsace-Lorraine

Rhein

Alternate Names

Holland : The Netherlands
Ypres : Iepers
Aerschot : Aarschot
Malines : Mechelen
Louvain : Leuven
Cologne : Köln
Aix la Chapelle : Aachen
Brussels : Bruxelles

From
Berlin

Legend

● Capital City
● Place of Interest
+++ Emily's Rail Journeys
···· Shipping route
— River
— Western Front 1914-18
—·· International borders, c.1914
- - Post war border

Pontarlier
Basel
Lausanne
Berne
Zurich
Geneva
Kienthal
SWITZERLAND

Scale:
0   75   150km
0   47   95miles

ITALY
To Rome Milan

AUSTRO-
HUNGARY

2. (left) Journeys taken by Emily Hobhouse 1915–16, showing the places she visited in Belgium, the approximate battle lines and position of Alsace-Lorraine. (Cartography by Catherine J. Griffiths, 2013)

3. (below) Central Europe, showing the Austria-Hungarian Empire and the position of Galicia and Serbia. In 1915 Emily Hobhouse was keen to go to Galicia, where there had been fighting with Russia and conditions were said to be very bad. She wished to investigate. Most of Galicia was Polish speaking and after the war it was transferred to an independent Poland. (Cartography by Catherine J. Griffiths, 2013)

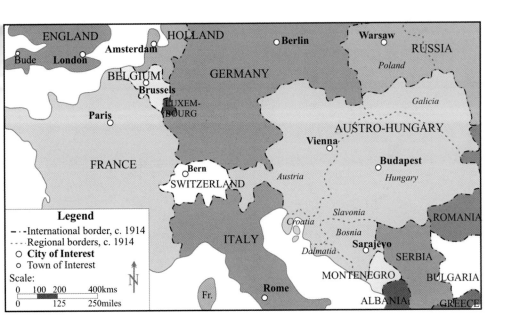

4. Emily. (Photograph from official German files 1916)

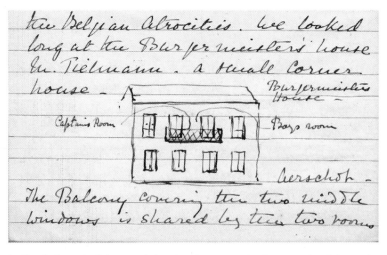

the Belgian Atrocities. We looked long at the Burgermeister's house M. Tielmann. a small Corner house —

Burgermeister's House —

Captains Room

Boys room

Aerschot —

The Balcony covering the two middle windows is shared by the two rooms

5. Sketch from Emily's Journal showing damage to the Burgermeister's house in Aerschott. See p. 71.

THE COMMISSION FOR
RELIEF IN BELGIUM.

№ 3, LONDON WALL BUILDINGS,
LONDON, E.C.

14th August, 1916.

Dear Miss Hobhouse,

I go home Westward every night
about six o'clock, and if it would
suit your convenience better I could
drop in at the Westminster Palace
Hotel about that time, any evening
you can suggest.

Yours faithfully,

Herbert Hoover

Miss Emily Hobhouse,
Westminster Palace Hotel,
S.W.

6. One of Emily's letters
from Herbert Hoover – the
future President of the
United States. See p. 147.

7. Bronze bust of Emily Hobhouse.

EMILY HOBHOUSE 1860-1926
RSA   4c
7.76—9
R
JOHAN HOEKSTRA   1976

8. Emily Hobhouse commemorated on
a South African stamp, 1976.

9. A facsimile of Herr von Jagow's reply from the German Foreign Office files. See p. 100 (Auswärtiges Amt means Foreign Office)

000264

you, you will find me at the Foreign Office this afternoon between 6 and 7 o'clock Hoping that this won't be too much Trouble for you, I remain

very sincerely your

10. Land's End by Caroline Trelawny, Emily's mother, circa 1845. Emily loved Cornwall and drew inspiration and strength from its landscape.

He spoke of Herr von Bülow and others in our Camps about whom they were anxious. I told him I thought there was not much to complain of materially in Ruhleben but that the men needed a mental and spiritual tonic. We discussed all this and then spoke of peace and the prospects of negotiation. He was very anxious for peace but very angry that the Chancellor's feelers put out had met only with insults. He ended by saying that if we would not make peace then they could go on and they would. He asked a good deal about the Labour and Peace movements in England and their strength and extent – but I had been too long away to be able to speak with certainty. He was an able man much younger than von Jagow, but lacking his gentleness and moderation.

I walked back in the sunny evening light – and finished packing and paying my bill etc. I could not forget von Stumm. He was angry and vehement – against his will inclining to the Military School – whose policy must come in if Bethmann Hollweg [the government] fails.

The Falkenhausens came and we supped in the hotel on eggs (me) fish (they). She was in tears poor girl, sick with grief – he quiet and calm. I hurried thro' and excusing myself to collect my things left them to themselves. Also I was looking out for Elisabeth Rotten who had promised to bring me boiled eggs. In the end we left the hotel a bit early and she had not come. I heard after she was only two minutes late – but I am glad because she would have had the precious eggs to eat. She had brought me chocolate and biscuits earlier. At the station Rieth turned up again. I am sure he was a spy, he had spies' eyes, small, piercing, wary, watchful – giving nothing, searching always. And he wasn't a gentleman. My Baron let out that his wife could not bear him and I knew she felt too his inferiority and probably knew he was a spy. Having nothing to conceal I did not mind. However on this occasion he was useful to talk to while the young couple took what might be their last farewell.

Then we left in the long midsummer evening and sped across the plain. We passed Wittenberg, notorious for its typhus [PoW] Camp, obviously an ill-chosen site, for the Elbe and tributaries wound about – the ground a dead level and pools and marshes seemed evident. I could see the camp and men walking about in it. And then a Zeppelin came into view – practising in the still, sunny air – a fine sight their Leviathan of the skies, swerving and dipping and diving and curvetting and above all dropping no bombs. A vision of the future therein. And dark fell and heavy with fatigue I slept soundly enough – and woke to exquisitely served coffee hot and fragrant at some town, I think not Stuttgart but one before that. It was later perhaps 9 a.m. when we reached Stuttgart and coiled round the picturesque town. Then on again through prettier country – where the crops of hay were being gathered in and the air grew ever warmer – on and on till we reached the frontier village of Singen. There the Swiss train would meet me and the Courier from Berne young Rosenberg take me across. But there were hours to wait. I had dinner in the little restaurant, there seemed plenty to eat. And had a wash in a ridiculously small outside lavatory and got rid of the extra clothing I had needed in the north. Then I sauntered out and sat on a bench in the dusty hot street, my Baron was hob-nobbing with the officers and had hinted we should be wise to keep apart. My money had lasted to a mark.

At last came the Swiss train and von Rosenberg. The Baron came and delivered me up – and much moved grasped my hand – 'Auf Wiedersehen' – a bow to the evidently astonished local Commandant – and I was whisked away and the wonderful visit was over. I thanked him, so I said, 'There are ways and ways of doing a thing and you have done it beautifully and with tact. My love to your wife, some day we shall meet again.'

And Germany will always live in my mind as I saw her those seventeen days – suffering – quiet – patient but calm and confident. I felt rather than knew that she could never be conquered. The whole country is at war there in a way that it is not even yet dreamed of in England.

It was sadly beautiful to watch – and awful to feel one was part of the enemy nation that was causing the wounds. One wanted to stretch forth ones arms and heal the wounds of soul and body. Peace, to help on Peace was the only way and I had that hope. My desire to get to London was great – my agitation lest I should be prevented very distressing, it affected my heart. I tried to keep calm ...

Correspondence Between Emily Hobhouse and Baron Gottlieb von Jagow, German Foreign Secretary

Excellence Baron von Jagow
18th June 1916

Dear Herr von Jagow[2]

Five or six years have passed since I used to meet you at Marchesa de Viti de Marco's house in Rome and much has happened since then to blot those calm days from our memory.

I believe, however, that I am indebted to you, ultimately, for this unprecedented privilege that has been granted to me of visiting Belgium and Berlin in wartime. I want to thank you with all my heart for this privilege.

It is my great and passionate desire to do all that a single individual can do, to draw our two countries together once more and to this end I believe (as far as my own country is concerned) a knowledge of the truth is the first step necessary. Hence, my desire to see Belgium, Ruhleben, etc.

Further, I believe it to be a point of supreme importance to be able to convey to the English Government my belief that Germany cannot be overcome by the food difficulty – if I can obtain sufficient data to support and justify that opinion.

It would, I fear, be unjustifiable to ask to see you personally in this stress of work and thank you by word of mouth as I should wish to do; but at any rate I do not like to be in Berlin without giving you this bare outline of my purpose and without sending a direct word of gratitude for your chivalrous understanding of my wishes.

Both in Berne and Brussels I have received the greatest kindness and I hope to carry home a point of view that shall have real weight and value.

I have the honour to be
Yours faithfully
Emily Hobhouse

Jagow's letter in reply is shown in plate 9 and transcribed below:

Auswärtiges Amt
Monday 19th [June 1916]

Dear Miss Hobhouse![3]

Many thanks for your kind letter. I was so glad to hear you still remember our meeting at Mesa. di Viti's.

Happy times!

It would give me great pleasure to see you and, if it suits you, you will find me at the Foreign Office this afternoon between 6 and 7 o'clock.

Hoping that this won't be too much trouble for you, I remain

Very sincerely yours

Jagow

June 20, 1916

Dear Herr von Jagow[4]

Thinking over our interview, I suddenly remembered that I failed to put before you one of the most important factors in the English political situation – one which you are hardly likely to know of, since it is studiously kept out of or distorted in the Times and kindred papers.

The Peace Movement in England (which developed amongst those who stood for our neutrality in 1914) is growing by leaps and bounds. It is not an insignificant movement nor is it confined to a body like the Independent Labour Party, but embraces men of all parties and class from Lord Loreburn and Lord Courtney and other people through the House of Commons down to the rank and file.

This movement is daily being reinforced by those who are weary of war or who have learnt to see this war in its true light and it is bringing constant pressure upon the government to begin negotiations for Peace. You can imagine how greatly this movement was helped by the noble speeches of your great Chancellor which in fact are a mighty weapon for its use.

Now, hitherto Asquith etc. has taken the line of ignoring this movement but I have recently heard that it was grown so powerful of late that they, the government, must reckon with it very soon.

Meanwhile, the replies to your Chancellor's speeches which read to you as insults are, I believe, Grey and Asquith's last efforts in what we call 'playing to the gallery'. The less insistent phrases are intended for you, the bombastic words are for their adherents not in England but amongst the Allies.

Please try and believe this and convey to Herr Bethmann Hollweg what we long to express to him, our deep gratitude and our determination to support him to the utmost.*

I have profound belief in personal contact and the wonderful way in which difficulties melt away when two people come face to face, finding after all that the points that unite are stronger than those that divide.

It was borne in on my mind last night how good it might be if you or one of your great statesmen wanted change of air and took it, say – at Scheveningen and if Grey or one of his more sympathetic colleagues like Lord Crewe or Lord Robert Cecil had a fancy to visit Holland and you met by chance upon the sands – talking first only as men, till a basis was found for the consideration of statesmen.

Such a plan seems to me more sensible than continued slaughter and if you agreed and wished I could make a similar suggestion to them in London.

If I presume in writing these thoughts, please forgive me.

My visit to Ruhleben is postponed till tomorrow so that I cannot now leave Berlin before Thursday.

I have the honour to be
Yours very sincerely
Emily Hobhouse

B[erlin] 20th June 16

Dear Miss Hobhouse![5]

Many thanks for your kind letter. I quite agree with you that eventual negotiations for peace would be facilitated by preliminary unofficial conversations. But if I am not mistaken about the dispositions of your leading men, I really don't see how any profit could derive at the present moment from such meeting as suggested in your

---

* This reflects the desire expressed in Emily's Journal (page 86) to keep the military out of politics. Bethmann Hollweg's eldest son was a Rhodes scholar at Oxford. He was killed in the first year of the war.

letter. The reception given to the Chancellor's speeches as well as many other sympshomes [*sic*] go a long way to show that any further step on our part in the direction of peace would only be considered in England as another proof of our inability to continue the war and would have, in consequence, the effect of giving a new encouragement to the war-party in your country.

If there is any possibility of realising your suggestion, it seems to me that it would be for England to move in the matter.

Thanking you once more for your kind visit.

Believe me

Very sincerely yours

Jagow

His Excellency Baron von Jagow

21st June, 1916

Dear Herr von Jagow:[6]

I quite agree that the proposal to meet privately which I suggested should not come from you.

My idea was that the suggestion should be made by me to the men at home and if by chance I found a willingness, I would try to let you know via Switzerland and Herr von Romberg.

You see, it would give me confidence in making the suggestion in England if I knew that you would not reject it on your side. That knowledge, however, would be for myself alone.

I feel sure my first work is to insist on the fact that Germany is quite able to go on with the war from all points of xxx [ileg] and that her desire for peace is based on reason and Humanity and not on lack of food, money or men. That truth when learnt should go far to clear the way.

I have seen Dr. Lewandowski today who has given me helpful and interesting facts about the health of the women and children.

Yours very sincerely

Emily Hobhouse

PS Scheveningen would be the place I should suggest to them in London.

B[erlin] 21st June 1916

Dear Miss Hobhouse![7]

Naturally I should not reject a proposal for informal conversations coming from England. But as I am afraid of misinterpretation, I ask you not to mention that I agreed to it in advance.

I am glad you received the impression here that we can't be starved out and that we are not at the end of our forces anyway.

Believe me

Very sincerely yours

Jagow

9

EMILY'S JOURNAL:
DISASTER AND THE
RETURN TO ENGLAND

At the Swiss frontier some difficulty was offered for the first time and the officer would not let us pass with the courier till he showed him my English passport. This franked me and mercifully was not stamped. This escort, as before, left me alone in my compartment and I was thankful for the rest. It was a long and very hot journey stopping at every station till we reached Zürich at about 7 p.m. There changing trains, in the crowd I lost my escort. Heat intense. I wired to the Kochers to meet me at Berne and arrived there half dead at 9.30 p.m. I had wired from Singen to Angelica [Balabanoff] to meet me at Zürich, but she never got the message. The Kochers, sweet people, met me and drove me to the Volkshaus where Phoebe had come with my boxes. We sat and talked and agreed I should spend Sunday afternoon in their garden resting if I did not get off. My desire was to leave next day for England.

Saturday, June 24th I went to the Consulate early to ask for a visé for England. Imagine my consternation when a long paper was handed to me with an immense and detailed list of questions to be filled in for myself and Phoebe. I sat down to write the replies till

I came to one which asked if one had been in 'Enemy territory since 1914'. Then I saw I should be obliged to tell my story to Grant Duff the British Minister, whom according to my written promise before leaving Berne, I had intended to call upon on leaving the Consul.

I finished Phoebe's papers and departing prepared to go to the English Legation – I was exhausted and very agitated lest I should be baulked in my desire to reach London and give my message of peace. My heart was palpitating violently, the more so coming back to the high Swiss altitudes. I went for a cup of strong black coffee and then took the tram to the Legation. The Interview was very entertaining and once begun I felt at ease and master of the situation.

I had been told that Mr Duff was ... really at present in a state of such excitement as hardly to be considered normal and the knowledge of this helped me to an understanding of how to deal with him. I treated him therefore like a nurse does a fever patient, or a fretful child. It succeeded. In outward appearance he lacked dignity and reminded me of the 'little cock-sparrow' giving itself airs. On my entrance, he did not offer to shake hands but motioned me to a chair with a lordly gesture and before I could make any remark he began: 'Miss Hobhouse, have you directly or indirectly by word or by letter been undertaking Peace propaganda? Have you attended any peace meetings, conferences or Congresses? Have you been consorting with Pacifists, Socialists or Germans.'

To this question which was longer and fuller than here appears I made no reply – but instead I said, when he paused for breath, 'Mr Duff, I have come up here this morning to take you into my confidence. I have been to Ruhleben Camp'. I fully thought the man would have had a fit – and taking advantage of his temporary paralysis I went calmly on to say 'and so I should be very glad if you will help me to get home'.

Then the fullness of his wrath fell upon me: 'You have been to Germany' – 'Enemy territory' – 'Without British permission' – 'you have broken the law', etc, etc. Then he drew a picture of my gruesome fate – how France would not let me pass – she would put me into prison, how Switzerland would not keep those France turned out – and as for England he was sure she would never let me land again! So I laughed a little and said I really did not think it was as bad as all that and asked what law I had broken; I was quite unaware that

I had broken any law. This put him in a difficulty, as he evidently could not conjure up any law to meet the case. So he flung out again in a burst of passion and I sat quiet till it was over. Then I remarked that I had thought he would like to hear about Ruhleben but he scornfully said he did not want to hear – he knew all about Ruhleben. So I said, 'Very good then I need not trouble you, but I know many in England from Lord Newton* downwards are anxious for details. When another burst of fury had subsided, I said: 'Mr. Duff, I know that there are many things that you and I look at from a very different point of view but one thing I am sure we have in common, and that is our desire for the honour and well being of England'. At this he became quite calm and childlike and said penitently, 'Well and what were your impressions of Ruhleben?' With this I plunged in and described everything, and shewed him samples of the bread I had brought and he was obliged to say, 'M looks fairly good' and at the end I said being in Germany I had became possessed of information that I felt it my duty to convey without delay to the British Government. 'And what,' said he, 'is the character of the information?' 'That Mr Duff,' I replied, 'is for the British Government.' He was silenced.

He said he must wire for instructions. I said, 'By all means, pray do.' Then he burst into a fresh and final tirade of anger – very forced and ridiculous to which I replied that I was content to leave it to Sir Edward Grey. I rose and he opened the door for me and amused me by putting both hands behind his back evidently regarding me as pitch – so I put up my hand cheerfully and said, 'Goodbye Mr Duff,' and perforce he had to meet it – doing so only with the extreme tips of his fingers and a face expressive of distaste and disdain. I was immensely tickled – the whole thing such a childish farce – and I came away feeling completely conqueror and sure as could be that I should get my pass.

But I was undoubtedly exhausted.

I forgot to say that the first thing that morning before going to the Consul I had gone to the German Embassy feeling it my duty to give an account of myself – and because I feared if I did not go there first

---

* Lord Newton was a long-serving parliamentarian who had taken on a voluntary war job of looking after internment camps and propaganda for the British Foreign Office. He had previously been Paymaster General in Asquith's government.

I might be forbidden later. Having to go by 11 a.m. to the Consulate I had very little time. I did not see von Schubert, but had a half of an hour with von Romberg, whose warning of the mental condition of Mr Duff proved most useful.

After the Legation I went to lunch and to rest which I needed badly. Frau Kocher and her husband came and with him I made an elaborate scheme of correspondence in case of need. He was, as ever, most thoughtful and kind. I had also help from Gertrude Woker. All this afternoon and the next day I must remain in suspense as to my fate.

Sunday morning, June 25th I was resting when Gertrude Woker came in to hear the news and tell hers and to promise to care for my papers and documents. I told her my plan of writing also to Dr Aletta Jacobs to tell her of my visit to Berlin and the possibility of a message having to be sent from London to Herr von Jagow and that correspondence via Switzerland was so uncertain I thought it better to safeguard matters by arranging to transmit a message also through her if necessary. Of course this necessity would only arise if I succeeded in reaching England – in seeing Sir Edward Grey and in laying my information and message before him. In my ignorance I did not know or realize that Governments, even when at deathgrips, have links through the Red Cross for instance and through neutral Embassies. This I learnt later – at the time I thought of them with an unbridged chasm between them and that for the fulfillment of my mission I must prepare and keep a link. Gertrude fully [agreed] though she knew only the bare outline – I felt I must tell no one in Berne except von Romberg. With all this in mind I had prepared a letter to Aletta Jacobs – very short which I read her and she thought it quite clear. I should, of course, only post it if I were certain of my passports. We parted, and after lunch I went as agreed to 25 Laupen Strasse to spend a quiet afternoon in the beautiful Kocher garden. I was so thankful to be still, and think, and to have my shaken body at rest. It soothed and calmed me. After tea towards 6 o'clock Baron von Romberg called on me there to say goodbye and to hear more in detail of my impressions in Germany. I spoke freely. He was very nice, very cordial and very much moved. He dropped the Ambassador and was purely and only the man. We talked till nearly dusk that midsummer evening. He told me, should my passports be denied me, to rely upon him to help me to Holland, I thanked him and said, 'I can't believe they will stop me,

I won't believe it.' He shook hands with warmth and unveiled feeling and left me. He had spoken very freely of Germany and of her attitude, her powers, her feeling. A good man I feel sure and a tremendously hard worker – and so sensitive!

I followed in the tram to the Volkshaus and dropped exhausted into bed.

Monday, June 26th Warm and misty damp, occasional showers. Everything sticky. I had my trunks half packed hoping for the best, and the moment the Consulate was open I was there to learn my fate. To my relief the visé was given without another word, nor anything to fill in, only the Consul badgered me a good deal with questions about Mrs Holbach and wanted her address. This I would not let out – it was not my business – and I told him definitely Mrs Holbach was a chance acquaintance merely, and I was in no sense her keeper – that she was living in Switzerland quietly with her husband and family and I could not understand why she should be worried. He dropped it and then said I must provide more photographs and that, though all else was complete, more photographs were necessary. The time was short. I pleaded – he was obdurate and I had to drag my tired, agitated body from shop to shop begging for a hasty snapshot likeness. It was 12.30 p.m. before I found one – was photoed and promised them by 2.30 p.m. Then I ventured to go and buy my tickets provisionally, got some lunch – sent Phoebe to the Wokers and Kochers with the news and worked on with the packing. I had barely time to run out and get an omelet and be at the photographers at the hour. Phoebe as usual tiresome, amusing herself in a shop, and keeping me waiting. A truly impossible girl! This delay on her part when every moment was of consequence and my fatigue and anxiety beyond words, added to my agitation. The photographs were given me in a large square envelope and I just put them into my green linen bag (the one Oliver gave me), which I always carried for passports and papers. I had also put into this bag after lunch my letter written the previous day to Dr. Aletta Jacobs and of which I have already spoken. And therein hangs a tale! As I have said I could not send it till absolutely sure of my departure and the French visé had still to be secured. I wanted also a lucid moment in which to read it over once more to assure myself it was *quite* clear – and so I had put it into this precious bag thinking that when Phoebe mounted this long flight to the Consul's office I could read it again while waiting in the vestibule below. As also I have said the day was warm and moist, everything was sticky and also alas! was the gum of this open letter or that of the large envelope containing my new photographs, or both. Arrived at the Consulate I sat down to get my breath and opened my bag to give Phoebe the photographs to take upstairs. At that moment the hall door opened and one of the officials of the office passed in from his luncheon. I bowed, made way for him to pass and said impulsively: 'May I hand you the photographs which I was asked to procure,' and gave him the packet. Phoebe followed him upstairs and I was left, quiet and alone, in the cool dim hall. Then I bethought me of my letter that this was the moment to read it over carefully. Imagine my horror to find on opening my bag that it was not there. I searched and searched again – all no use. I felt so sure I had put it there. Could it have been left on my toilet table after all? I went through every action of the day but could come to no other conclusion. I was sure 'twas in my bag – yet it wasn't – so it must be in hotel. I waited endlessly – Phoebe did not come down. Why such delay? The passports had been entirely ready with the exception of gumming on the photo and I feared missing the hour at the French Consul. After an interminable interval Phoebe came down – with the passports – and horrors, in her hand my lost letter saying in her cool detached way the official said he thought this 'was not meant for them'. I exclaimed – and she too seemed rather put about – said there was nobody there but they had kept her a long time – they had seemed to be very pleased about something and chuckled together and they had gone into an inner room and locked the door which they had never done before and she heard the typing and she said she thought they had copied it. In my own mind I had no doubt, and that became certainty when I drew out the letter – saw that the sheets were soiled with typing ink and pinned together.

The man was a cad! It was almost the last straw on a day of great strain – not that I felt I had done anything but what was right and under the cirčes sensible – but I feared that either they might stop me or else try to discredit me in London and so destroy my mission.

It was therefore very dejectedly that I went up to the French Consulate. Here I encountered considerable difficulties – French officials are very snappy and irritable. My papers had to pass before four separate men – the last one demanded more photographs but I told him I had none. The English Consul had them all, five besides the one pasted in. He was high-handed, said it was the rule and he must have at least four. I was sorry but could not give him what I had not got. He was rude and it was long before he would let me go. At last he consented and utterly exhausted I came out – sent Phoebe back to finish the packing and went to get the sleeper tickets.

We made a hurried supper and so to the station in fairly good time. Fortunately Frau Kocher came to see me off and, hurriedly, I was able to tell her of this contretemps of my stolen letter – the results of which I feared might be serious for my work. When we started Phoebe told me the clerk from the Passport Office was on the platform and she believed watching us. The reason for this Espionage I learned later. At the moment I thought it was to see who saw me off and who my friends in Berne might be.

Once the train was off my anxiety was relieved and I felt sure no hindrance would be placed in my reaching London. I knew Grant Duff's wire had been answered saying I was to be allowed to pass and that Sir Ed Grey knew through him that I had information I wanted to give and I felt therefore certain I was under the protection of the Foreign Office. The men I detest and fear are the underlings who seem to crop up and come to the fore in wartime (just as in South Africa) and who are always suspicious unreasonable arbitrary and invariably *Cads*.

As we neared Neuchâtel and I came to myself a bit I realized that once over the border I should no longer be able to correspond freely with anyone in Switzerland and I felt I must write at once to the British Consul and tell him I had discovered that my letter had been tampered with and if he could assure me it was not and he must write to me in London at once. I told him how painful it was to me to think that his office contained men who could do such an ungentlemanly deed and it made me ashamed of the British Consulate in Berne. That any man would open and read and copy a private letter handed him by a mistake was the act of a dishonorable Cad. I further said that whatever information it contained could and would be of no use unless with the consent of the British Government and now none at all as of course I cancelled it at once on finding out their treachery.

This I wrote in pencil in the train and posted at Neuchâtel and I felt calmer when it was done. The letter which was copied by them was almost word for word as follows:

To Dr. Aletta Jacobs – 1507 Koninginneweg, Amsterdam.

Dear Friend,

I am leaving Switzerland tonight and so shall not have any further chance of writing to you freely.

You know I have been to Berlin and have seen members of the Govmt there. When I get back to London it may be necessary for me to send a reply to a kind of message I have to carry. The posts via Switzerland are so very uncertain that I think it would be better and surer by Holland. So if you get a postcard from me beginning as above but which does not seem to have any meaning for you will you be so kind as to take it (not send it by post) to the German Ambassador at the Hague and ask him to forward it to Herr von Jagow.

Forgive my writing in great haste.

Yrs. etc. EH

These are almost the words and exactly the substance of what I wrote. Needless to say I never had explanation or apology from the Consul – who poor man (a Swiss Subject too) was I well knew not himself in fault. Later I learned that Captain Binns an attaché at the British Legation was the caddish hero of this brilliant war exploit. A lady who stayed at the same hotel came to England and told me all about it. She said Captain Binns told everyone – made no secret of it – and she herself could actually repeat to me the main parts of the letter. She evidently disliked Capt Binns very much and had snubbed him a good deal.

Anyhow he bragged a great deal saying how delighted he was – that they had 'tried in vain to find anything against Miss Hobhouse.' Later he came to England bringing with him the copy of the letter which he appears to have taken to the Foreign Office and I believe that and that only explained the conduct of Lord Robert Cecil later in the summer and inspired the attack upon me in Parliament. This lady told me how she heard me often discussed by groups of these young attachés and officers and how one day after they had been libelling and slandering me for my work in South Africa and again now – Major Dansey(?) suddenly spoke: 'After all Miss Hobhouse has not been half so bad in this war as she was in the Boer War and the worst of it is she was damn right!' My friend said, 'I left it at that, thinking his words, he being an older and serious man and head of the Intelligence Department at the War Office, would have the best effect.'

But all this is a digression to finish the story of the letter about which I may hear more in the future. Still I feel it was the only commonsense thing to have done considering that I was unaware that Warring Governments had other means of communicating.

We were soon at Pontarlier and had to be scrutinized anew. Just before arriving there I had some talk with an English lady in the train and learnt that if one stayed the night in Paris it would necessitate viséing etc again – but this would not be required if one went straight through.

My examination at Pontarlier was very close. Of course we were both stripped to the skin – an affair I am getting used to and always make light of. Then my bag and papers were opened and plain writing pads taken – not written upon. They said these were prohibited. My passport – or some words on it, I know not what – caused considerable uncertainty and one after another was called to examine it. I sat in outward tranquility and unconcern and inward trepidation awaiting the issue. At last a Superior was called and he scrutinized it and me, then finally banged the book down on the table with a 'Sans arrêt'* and I was free. We crept out in the dark and found our sleeper and some much needed coffee, though indeed perspiration was streaming down my face with exhaustion and fatigue rather than heat. I was so thankful for the quiet darkness of the sleeper and the unbroken journey through the night – with Paris and a good wash to greet the morning.

At the Gare de Lyons I found a 'Cooks' man to help me – feeling him well worth his weight in francs and he and Phoebe went off to claim the luggage while I ordered coffee and rolls. How refreshing it was, though alas! quantity and quality not what it used to be! Then Phoebe returned and when she had finished breakfast he found us a cab driven by a great-grandfather! and told us of a quiet Hotel (London and New York) close in front of our next station Gare St. Lazare. A nice, quiet, very small little Inn. I took a room for the inside of the day (6frs!!) and washed. Then I sallied forth to Cooks office in Plâce de l'Opera to secure tickets, and berths from Havre. This done and no

---

* Although the passport was stamped 'Sans arrêt', 'without stopping', it was an acknowledged fact that this journey required a day in Paris.

difficulty encountered except uncertainty itself a sufficiently disagree-
able element of travel I took a cab and drove to Faubourg S. Honoré
to find the le Foyers. The day was still young, though I had not realized it, having forgotten time and space. It was barely 10 a.m., early
for a call, and Madame le Foyer was in her peignoir and M Lucien le
Foyer in bed and asleep. I was disappointed wanting much to see him,
but she received me and I talked long with her. Then I drove to Quai
Debilly and to my joy found both Madame Duchêne and her daughter. They begged me to take an early lunch with them and meanwhile
I told them all my adventures and heard their news and outlook. Their
movement was growing steadily though slowly and silently. All had to
be done by hand and not through the post. The Socialist Deputies –
Brizon, Raffin Dugens and Blanc – were brave and had done nobly
but they were not the men who carried most weight. Nevertheless
'twas a beginning.

I returned to the Hotel and Phoebe and the luggage – we posted
photos and some special papers – and went across to the Station.
The train started about 4 p.m. and it must have been about 6.30
p.m. when we reached Havre. Here again I encountered difficulty
as the passengers from the crowded train filed through the Passport
Office. My name seemed known and the passport was handed from
one to another. I was looked up under letter H in a card index and
found to be No. 85. This 'quatre vingt-cinq' was shouted aloud and a
Portfolio was brought full of typewritten sheets. It was obviously my
character and history – the wicked history of a Pacifist!!! There was
consternation while I stood imperturbable and unconcerned. I could
not believe I had got so far to be stopped at last. A white-headed old
man was summoned from an inner room who scrutinized me – all
were uncertain how to act when fortunately this man asked if no
English Official were there. A young man at once rose, looked at the
passport and at me and with alacrity and extreme readiness as of a
person expecting to see me, said 'O Yes, Miss Hobhouse? By all means
– pass this way. Your maid? Certainly. Quite in order etc.' And so again
I knew I was under the protection, at any rate for the time, of our
Foreign Office. But what was to come?

If I had only known it – I was more than safe – for Captain Binns
later told my friend that their one idea was to get me safely back
to England – that they had feared that my discovery that my letter

had been tampered with, could make me afraid to go home and that I should stay in Switzerland and give them trouble.

Needless to say such an idea never occurred to me. I felt I had a mission to fulfill – and as for the letter, it being merely a common-sense arrangement in regard to that mission, I had no guilty conscience about it at all. It was the only wise thing to do. But I was told that was the official fear in Berne that I should remain there and that was why Captain Binns came down to the station to assure himself that I really did go.

It never occurred to me to want to stay in Switzerland, but it appears that the Legation there prefers to have no English pacifists so near Enemy territory and indeed Enemy residents. I found indeed great suspicion of some English pacifists and semi-pacifists such as Mrs Holbach and others who were watched and plagued by the Legation.

From the Passport Office there was a long distance to the Docks and no cabs to be found. Finally an open tram took the passengers and hand luggage and we were promised the registered baggage would come later. It was some way – the streets were crowded with British Tommies. I could not help comparing them with the German masses of troops so lately seen. These by comparison seemed so slim and so white and so boyish looking – reedy many of them – the Germans shorter, broader, more robust. Ours so trim in newest outfits, the Germans less trim and more worn in appearance.

With difficulty we struggled through and found the ship and berths. 'Twas well I had wired to reserve from Paris. We found the vessel would not start till near midnight – and meanwhile the boxes must be found. For all this sort of thing Phoebe was useless. I had myself to go again to the quay and stand for hours in the great shed and watch while wagon after wagon brought the baggage to be sorted.

All Red X trunks were passed without delay or trouble. It was nearly 11 p.m. before I had spied my three articles and got them placed together and then found a weary official – a woman – to open them. But at last this terrific day was over and I was free to go and rest. Tired out, we both soon fell asleep – only to be awakened by a loud-voiced Red X woman who bounced into my cabin insisting it was hers – which it was not. This, as usual with a sudden awakening, gave my heart such a shock that I had a restless night though the sea was calm as a lake.

Wednesday, June 28th We were docked in good time at Southampton and by 7 a.m. on the quay looking for coffee – a rapid pass through the customs and London by 11 a.m. No such luck. I could see delay writ large on all sides and saw we must be content to take things leisurely. I sent two telegrams: one to Sir Edward Grey 'Arrived Southampton. Proceed to London. Shall await your kind instructions in the Westminster Palace Hotel.' The other wire was to the Hotel reserving rooms for myself and Phoebe. N.B. These wires were all censored. I did not at the moment think of that, but as matters turned out the openness of my movements was all to the good. We drank our coffee – very bad stuff. Then, as for once benches were provided for the unfortunate waiting hours for tardy Officials and Officialism, we sat down on the last bench to abide our turn. I found at once I was expected and my name known and I prepared to meet it all with frankness and good humor, though burning to hurry on to London. My experience of Wartime officials in South Africa stood me in good stead in these days. The great thing is never to resist in any way – or show the slightest objection to the unpacking of anything however treasured. Keep smiling and civil … My orders to Phoebe were to remember this and to reply with exact truth to anything she was asked …

10

THE CITADEL

eanwhile, at the British Foreign Office in London, the health and welfare of the Foreign Secretary, Sir Edward Grey was of prime concern. His sight had been deteriorating. He wore dark glasses and had to take long breaks from the office. Although the war was at full ferocity, apparently no attempt was made to replace him. He was, however, ably supported by his Parliamentary Undersecretary, Lord Robert Cecil, a son of the former Prime Minister, Lord Salisbury. Cecil, who was trained as a barrister, was also Minister for the Blockade and, as such, had a place in the Cabinet. He enjoyed parliamentary work and answered questions for Grey in the House of Commons. (Questions in the House of Lords were answered by the Lord President of the Council, Lord Crewe.) In mid-July Grey was to receive the title of Viscount. Grey and Cecil worked hand in hand and ultimately it was Cecil who was responsible for actions concerning Emily. Cecil was considered broad-minded but, although he supported Millicent Fawcett in her bid for votes for women, his actions towards her suggest he believed that women should be subservient. He would almost certainly have been aware that Millicent Fawcett considered Emily Hobhouse a traitor. Emily was not subservient.

The Foreign Office in those days was an all-male preserve, although as a war measure, there may have been a trickling of women typists. There was a rigidness about Foreign Office dealings – Cecil liked to keep it that way. Its insistence on conducting all its business with other countries through diplomatic channels was both a strength and a weakness.

Grey had brought England into the war in 1914. Now it seems almost certain that peace could have been had in 1916 if Germany was sincere in its willingness to evacuate Alsace-Lorraine, as was said, and if something could have been done to stop this terrible build-up of armaments. Cecil, at the beginning of the war, had joined the Red Cross and on a visit to France that autumn had dined with the British commander Sir John French and his staff. French felt the Germans knew they were beaten and Britain should only ask for the return of Alsace-Lorraine and the restoration of Belgium in peace talks.[1] (At the other extreme Fritz Fischer in *Griff nach der Weltmacht* said Chancellor Bethmann Hollweg would have insisted on acquisition of the Longwy-Briery basin, near Metz in France, economic and military control over Belgium and a share of Persian oilfields for Germany.[2])

Emily Hobhouse had returned to England with four main objectives: first to get peace talks moving so as to avoid further bloodshed, second to obtain the release of civilian internees on foreign soil, third to get better food and supplies to the people of Belgium, and fourth to discuss the food position in Germany. Her Boer War reputation had brought her many friends in high places, but also many enemies who (although she had been proved right) had not forgotten what they considered as slights against the integrity of their government. The establishment had been rocked, their comfort space had been invaded. They had not forgiven her.

On arrival in London instead of seeing the Foreign Secretary, as she desired, Emily was summoned to New Scotland Yard for a grilling by Basil Thomson, Chief of the Criminal Investigation Department, Metropolitan Police, and liaison with the War Office and Admiralty Counter Intelligence Sections.[3]

Dr Diane Clements Kaminski* in her PhD thesis *Emily Hobhouse – The Radicalization of a Ministering Angel* says that since Grey had not answered her wire of 28 June, Emily wrote to him the next day, requesting a brief interview with him or Lord Crewe. She wanted to see one of them before she went to Scotland Yard and stressed that she would 'not feel happy until

---

* I am grateful to Dr Diane Clements Kaminski for introducing me to the government side of events, which she included in her PhD Thesis at the University of Connecticut. Kaminski did far more work in sifting through the Foreign Office files than I have been able to do.

I have told you all I have learnt,' and that 'it was only in the interests of our distracted world that she asked for this favour …'[4]

But the Foreign Office was in no hurry. It was waiting for the Scotland Yard report.

Thomson was aware of Evelyn Grant Duff's comments, had seen the copy of Emily's letter to Aletta Jacobs, the original of which, still unsigned, had been forwarded to Aletta Jacobs in Holland. The full text of the letter is as follows:

24th June /16

Dear Friend,

I hope, all being well, to leave Switzerland and go home on the wings of the wind, and ere leaving must write you once more freely because from England that will not be possible.

Listen – to business; I returned last night from a trip through Belgium and Germany. I have been to Berlin and seen von Jagow, whom I knew in old days. From this, much I hope may develop. I am to keep open a line of communication with him. Will you help? – saying nothing.

If you have a letter from me (or a card) from home, beginning as above 'Dear Friend' and signed by me – but either elusive or with not much meaning for you, will you put it into an envelope, but do not post it – take it to the Ambassador at the Hague, to forward urgently. If, through the same hand, any word or letter should come back to be forwarded to me, will you re-write it, if necessary in your own hand and sign it with your name, unless it should reach you from the Legation in a form in which it could be forwarded. But a postcard is better.

Gertrude Woker has been such a dear. I am too exhausted to write, but want you to know that Frau Ragaz and Mlle Gobat have returned from Stockholm very disgusted with affairs there – and say Rosika has gone home, for which they are sorry, since she has such a capacity. Dr. Aked seems a firebrand. Emily Balch is there and I hope she may pull the thing together.*

---

* Clara Ragaz and Marguerite Gobat were Swiss pacifists. Rosika Schwimmer, Dr Aked and Emily Greene Balch had all travelled to Sweden on Henry Ford's *Peace Ship*. Rosika was a vice chair of the International Committee of Women for Permanent Peace. Emily Greene Balch, a future Nobel Prize winner, was also associated with it. Dr Aked was a Baptist minister.

Everything is at its worst and this great battle is preparing. Thousands on both sides have to meet Death in July – or sooner.

Too tired to write.

I am establishing here also a line of communication, but posts are so uncertain across France that I think a duplicate line necessary.

With best love.[5]

Grant Duff had said he believed that this letter was the key to an international pacifist intrigue. He said that Emily had been staying in Berne with Gertrude Woker (which she hadn't actually – but used her address), and said Gertrude Woker was 'a militant pacifist well known to me as one of the most aggressive women in Switzerland'[6] and that the letter showed that Emily had arranged a code with the Germans. Further he believed Emily's pacifist activity to be subversive. One undersecretary at the Foreign Office agreed and said: 'This (letter) seems quite sufficient to justify interning Miss Hobhouse; and that even more drastic action might be taken.'[7]

Basil Thomson reported to his chief at the Metropolitan Police, C.F. Dormer, that Emily had given him a 'pretty clear picture' of her movements in Germany and Belgium, where she 'formed the opinion that the blockade was responsible for heavy infant mortality etc., exactly the sort of conclusions the Germans desired her to form'. She thought the prisoners, whom she interviewed at Ruhleben, were generally well treated though a number of them were suffering mental strain:

Her conclusions, of course, are quite immaterial, but I gathered in conversation that her talk with von Jagow included the usual discussion about Peace terms, and in that respect I think it probable that the Germans regard her as an unofficial peace emissary, from whose visit some results may be expected. I did not press her on the subject of the conversation, because she evidently preferred to communicate this to Sir Edward himself, or to someone delegated by him.

Up to a point she was evidently speaking the truth. I am expecting today or tomorrow a draft of a letter that she wrote to von Jagow from Switzerland, in her handwriting, which has come into our agent's hands but what she did omit to tell me (a fact that came into my hands after the interview) is that she was given an address in Amsterdam** to

---

** Thomson's facts were not correct or he would have seen that it was Emily who provided the address for Dr Jacobs, not Jagow, nor the German Foreign Office.

which she is to communicate when she wishes to write to von Jagow. Probably it will be possible to intercept the letter, but one cannot be sure, and therefore she ought to be treated with great reserve. At the same time I do think that it might be well for her to see the Foreign Office.'[8]

When Emily returned from New Scotland Yard she found a reply from Sir Edward Grey's Private Secretary dated 29 June, to inform her that he would not be able to see her on the 30th. He said: 'Sir Edward will be glad if Miss Hobhouse will communicate in writing the tenour of the information which she desires to give.'[9]

So she wrote on 1 July 1916:

Dear Sir Edward Grey,[10]

I only received today the kind note of your Private Secretary of June 29. I write to assure you that I bear no message from von Jagow and am in no way an Emissary of the German Government, a thing which I am sure would not be acceptable to you. It is simply that owing to the chance of old acquaintanceship I had a long and intimate conversation with him, easy and devoid of all official character – of the kind that gives one deep glimpses.

Afterwards it came to me a certainty that it was my duty – if you permit – to convey to you the gist of that talk for the day might come when it might be of great use to you.

One cannot convey such things by letter, therefore I have ventured to beg the honour of an interview.

I have the honour to be

Yrs Obediently

Emily Hobhouse

While she waited for Grey's reply to this letter, the Foreign Office had received Thomson's summary of his 30 June interview. Thomson now added: 'she has mentioned our offensive'. He was alarmed at her general lament about continuing war deaths.[11] (The names of the dead were printed daily in *The Times*. The Battle of the Somme was about to start. There were 57,000 British and Commonwealth casualties on the very first day – 1 July 1916 – so these lists could be very long.)

Thomson's position further changed when he received the copy of Emily's letter to Jagow (this letter is not preserved in British Foreign Office files but is available from German Foreign Office records). As Emily kept drafts or copies of many of her more important letters, this was likely to have been obtained by the British agent from Emily's maid – which would, of course, have been classic.

Bern, Schweiz
June 25 /16

To His Excellency
Dear Herr von Jagow,[12]
Grant Duff was very angry but I soothed him as one does a child and I think he will let me go. Under the new French regulations the fact of my visit had to come out – otherwise he had no idea of it.

The post is so uncertain now via France, that I think it wise to arrange a duplicate line of communication via Holland. I have a reliable friend there whom I have instructed to deliver any letter or postcard she receives from me worded allusively, to the German Minister at The Hague to be forwarded to you. If this postcard spoke of Edward or Edward's brother, you would know it meant Grey or one of his colleagues. Should you wish to send me any word in reply, she could send it to me instructed by your Minister.

Most important matters have nowadays to be written in duplicate for so much is lost.

She is absolutely reliable (but of course I have told her nothing).

Dr Aletta Jacobs, 158 Koninginneweg, Amsterdam

Though it may be true that men as a whole keep secrets better than women, yet some women can keep a secret better than any man.

Very sincerely Yours
Emily Hobhouse

Dormer now told the Foreign Office that 'the Police are now asking the Home Office to intern her, as being in communication with enemy subjects, and in the circumstances he [Thomson] thinks the FO should not see her'.[13] But at the Home Office, where Sir John Simon had been succeeded by another distinguished politician, Herbert Samuel, it was not thought necessary to intern Emily nor to take other measures.

11

DIARY, JULY 1916

For just sixteen days Emily kept a diary, something she was never keen to do. She preferred to write a journal or to tell her story in letters to her friends.

Nearly all the people Emily met and mentioned in the Diary, were Members of Parliament or prominent in other fields. Many were members of the Union of Democratic Control (UDC), formed at the beginning of the war by a group of Liberal MPs and others who believed that secret diplomacy had led to the outbreak of war. Among these, in particular, were E.D. Morel, who was said to have great organising abilities and had previously sought to limit the powers of King Leopold II of Belgium over the Belgian Congo; Arthur Ponsonby, a son of Sir Henry Ponsonby Queen Victoria's Private Secretary, a former diplomat who had considerable inside knowledge; Charles Trevelyan, who had held parliamentary office; and Charles Buxton. Other members were R.W. Outhwaite and Arnold Rowntree. J. Ramsay MacDonald, the future Prime Minister, and Norman Angel were among the founders. These people were all proponents of a negotiated peace. Lord Courtney was a sympathiser. Emily's brother, Leonard Hobhouse, who had been such a support to her in the Anglo-Boer War, was not a member of the group.

The first two pages of the Diary are missing. Perhaps Emily tore them out herself as she waited in the Westminster Palace Hotel for an answer to her wire to Sir Edward Grey. She said she felt very shaken by her visit to New Scotland Yard. One can imagine that her heart was playing her up:

Saturday, July 1st I was strangely relieved after my examination at New Scotland [Yard] was over, and the terrible palpitations of my heart subsided. Mr Ponsonby was unfortunately out of town. Still I could not shake off the impression of Martial Law and the idea of being watched. I called on the Devonports* but found they had just left for the weekend. Called also on Lord Courtney and had a fairly satisfactory talk with him, urging secrecy for the present. He looked very thin and ill, and seemed too weak for me to tell him all I wished.

In the evening I walked across to Mrs J.R. Green** and told her the position. As regards Ruhleben Camp she suggested I should lunch with her next day to meet Mrs Pope Hennessy who is on a Government Commission connected with the Red Cross for the care of our prisoners in Germany. Accepted gratefully. I urged Secrecy – she replied she was 'loaded up with Secrets' and promised. [So the weekend was not yet over and Emily was already pursuing her second objective – to obtain the release of civilian prisoners of war.]

Sunday, July 2nd Part of Abbey Service – tiring to my back. To lunch with Mrs Green. Found on arrival Mrs Pope Hennessey and her husband the Major – both already in full possession of my Secret. (Oh Mrs Green!) Found her very bitter and antagonistic. He very nice – Just off for Mesopotamia. She suggested I should go and visit their office in 18 Carlton House Gardens and we fixed Wednesday morning. I found her very difficult to talk to, but we agreed that the trouble in the Civilian Camp was mental primarily, and from her I first learned what I suspected, that a similar state of things obtained among the German prisoners in our Civilian Camps of Knockaloe, Alexandra Palace, etc. We agreed that the only sensible policy was the complete break up of the Camps – she of course imagined that only Germany was to blame for hindering this. I, on the other hand could assure her

---

* Lord Devonport who was to become Minister of Food Control, was the first Chairman of the Port of London Authority and founder of the International Stores.
** Mrs J.R. Green had helped Emily after the Anglo-Boer War in setting up Home Industries in South Africa.

that in the Foreign Office at Berlin it was asserted that our government put difficulties in the way.

Coming home looked at my little old house in Cowley Street – empty again. A fatality rests on that house.

Monday, July 3rd Mr Ponsonby called early. His visit was a great relief to me. I told him much but not the crème de la crème – upon which, however, he advised me how to act in regard to the Foreign Office. He was sympathetic and encouraging and asked to be allowed to tell the UDC Executive and arrange for me to meet them for a talk. In the evening Mr Outhwaite came and we had a good long chat.

Tuesday, July 4th Phoebe left. Her departure a true relief. She left everything in very bad condition. At 2 p.m. came Mr Charles Trevelyan, who had meantime, however, heard my news from Arthur Ponsonby. Still, we had a nice talk.

Wednesday, July 5th The Abbey – then to 18 Carlton House Gardens to Mrs Pope Hennessy. Saw also Mrs Livingstone and Sir Lewis Mallet. Found Mrs Hennessy as before, very brusque and 'difficile'. Mrs Livingstone more sympathetic and urged I should go with her on a tour to see the English Camps, Knockaloe and Alexandra Palace. Mrs H proposed arranging for me to see Lord Newton at once and telephoned there and then. The answer came he could see me at once, therefore I broke away, took a taxi and drove to the Foreign Office. Lord Newton was very nice, unofficial in mind and manner – open – agreed with me about the Camps – acknowledged same state of affairs here in England – desired complete exchange – was aware Germany had proposed this a year ago – said Kitchener had stood in the way.[*] 'These naval and military fellows,' he said, 'always make difficulties; they are narrow and one-ideaed and know nothing'. He thought (as I suggested) that the matter could be arranged easily enough by unofficial hands, and proposed that I should myself write to von Jagow and get the thing done. He said he could get it sent via USA Embassy, but it would have to be submitted to the Cabinet. I said I was quite agreeable to that. He said this must be kept quite private. I went home and wrote the letter and sent to him for this purpose.

---

[*] To Lord Newton's credit he had done a complete change around. In May he had considered such action as hers 'perfectly monstrous'.

At 3.30 that afternoon Mr Buxton came to see me – a very charming personality. He was busy about a Memorial for Negotiations, and I signed his paper. He arranged for his wife to come and see me later.

At 6.30 p.m. came Captain Bennett who was delightful and told me he had just completed translation of the German White Book on Belgium Atrocities. Asked me to lunch to meet his wife – counselled speaking to Lord Northcliffe who he said was pessimistic about the war.

At the Red Cross Headquarters Sir Lewis Mallet ran off a letter (5 July) to Sir Horace Rumbold** at the Foreign Office. It started with a flourish: 'Miss Hobhouse, pro-Boer and pro-German, called upon me this morning to my horror.'[1] (It is interesting that even though fourteen years had lapsed since the end of the Anglo-Boer War the term 'pro-Boer' was still used against Emily in a derogatory sense, regardless of what she had done to help the people, and that responsible diplomats should feel free to use name-calling in this way. As Emily had explained much earlier, being pro-Boer – having sympathy for them – certainly did not mean that one was anti-British. The same could be said of 'pro-German'.)

Guy Locock an assistant undersecretary at the Foreign Office, was intrigued by it and wrote to Sir Lewis Mallet: 'What else did the mischievous Miss Hobhouse say?'[2] In reply Mallet told Rumbold on 10 July that Miss Hobhouse was careful to speak favourably of the material conditions at Ruhleben and stressed that, though Germans had intended no mistreatment, the captivity was having a depressing, even maddening, effect on many men.

At that time Emily had apparently produced her plan for the exchange of all British and German civilians over military age who wished to go and for sending the remainder to a neutral country where normal life could be resumed. (This would have been the plan agreed with Stumm in the German Foreign Office.)

Lord Newton noted in his diary:

Miss E. Hobhouse, who has been lately at Ruhleben and gives very bad account. Wants to write to Jagow and propose exchange: told her

---

** Both Sir Lewis Mallet and Sir Horace Rumbold were career diplomats. Horace Rumbold was later to replace Grant Duff as minister in Switzerland.

to w[rite] and send letter for me to see, and that I would ask if it might go. Afterwards sent it to me; showed it to R. Cecil and Drummond, who thought it would not do ...

Afternoon, debate on Ruhleben. Just before making statement heard that reply had just arrived and that it was not categorical refusal ... Am being denounced in Harmsworth press as being too pro(?) Germany. Germans in note say they want whole of 26,000 here for our 4,000! According to Miss H. condition of Ruhleben people horrible ... [3]

The difference in numbers was because there were, according to the 1911 census, over 50,000 Germans living in Britain. Some had been there for generations. Not all were interned.[4]

It was on another matter that Lord Newton sent Emily a formal and private note the next day. Emily had asked him about her third objective – better food for Belgium:

Foreign Office

Private

July 6 1916

Dear Miss Hobhouse,[5]

I have nothing personally to do with Belgium, and perhaps you had better write to Lord Robert yourself. I will tell him, when I next see him, that you wish to speak to him.

You will probably have noticed that, since I saw you, the Germans have sent a reply about the exchange of civilians, which gives ground for hope of an eventual agreement.

In view of this, I feel sure that the authorities here will not be in favour of private communication on the subject, on the ground of causing further complications.

In that event, shall I send the letters back to you or shall I destroy them?

Yrs very truly

Newton

At the same time Emily had written another letter to Sir Edward Grey:[6]

5th July 1916

Dear Sir Edward Grey,

Since writing to you last Saturday I bought a copy of Hansard to read up debates – and in especial your speech of May 24th.

With profound feeling I read these words of yours:–

'The fact is the Allies are not beaten, and are not going to be. The first step towards peace will be when the German Government recognize that fact.' p. 2204

Now quite by chance I happen to know that the Hansard verbatim report of that debate was in the Foreign Office of Berlin; I myself however had not read it owing to the vicissitudes of travel.

But – reading it now – it seems to explain to me a certain insistence with which von Jagow repeated: 'The English are not beaten. It is true we Germans have had great victories, but we have also had great defeats. The English may have had no great victories but on the other hand have sustained no great defeats. We know full well the English are not beaten.'

The words struck me at the time and stand out clear in my brain, though perhaps I did not at the moment grasp their full import, and certainly did not know what now seems plain that they were a kind of reply to those words of yours.

Do please if you can find time let me see you and tell you all that passed for it weighs upon my mind.

Emily's requests went unheeded. In fact it had been decided at the Foreign Office that no one should see her.[7] So all Emily's reasonableness had come to nothing.

Lord Newton continued in his diary on 6 July: 'Discussion about German note & Ruhleben. R Cecil wants to intern everyone in neutral country.... Heard from Miss Hobhouse. Seems all right.'

He wrote to her from the Foreign Office that same day:[8]

Dear Miss Hobhouse

I am much obliged for your note. I think that I can safely undertake to dispose of the letter, fire or no fire!

Yrs vy truly

Newton

Thursday, July 6th Took my letter to the Foreign Office and walking back met Emeline Pethrick Lawrence. She asked me questions that shewed at once she knew of my visit to Germany and told me that Mrs Swanwick had told them at the Women's International League. I felt cross and saw the difficulty of keeping a Secret. She invited me to drive with her and I accepted. At 4.30 p.m. went to call on Mr Morel at UDC [Union of Democratic Control] Office and arranged [to talk at] a meeting of Exve for Tuesday – then on to St Clements Inn making a detour to see the Margaret Macdonald Memorial in Lincoln's Inn Fields. A pleasant tête-à-tête dinner with Emeline Lawrence (he away). She sympathetic and burning for information, little of which I could give her. Taxied back to the Hotel, she going to a meeting close by.

Friday, July 7th Margaret Clark came early but I was horribly exhausted and not able to talk to her as I wished. Very hearty and longing to know everything. Then to lunch with Bennetts in Chester Terrace. Mrs B. perfectly charming but I told her nothing as a stranger was there. When I got home callers came and at 5.30 p.m. Sylvia Parkhurst who shared my eggs tea with me and then was put to rest on my bed while we talked. She went on to speak at a meeting and I had Ravelli [a young pianist friend from South Africa] to tell me all his doings.

Saturday, July 8th No note or recollection of what happened that day. Correspondence. Dined at Bennetts and met Lady Barlow who was full of a scheme for taking her children to America.

Sunday, July 9th Kate Courtney called. When gone, came Dr Markel with his car who took me to lunch with him as previously arranged. Found him and his wife in a charming house with many rooms given over to work for the prisoners and stores for them. Mrs Markel very sweet – semi-invalid. Talked long – so sympathetic – then he drove me to the Courtneys where, however did not effect much as people kept coming in – Drakes, Fisher, Williams, etc so I came away. Expected Nell [another South African friend] that evening but she did not arrive.

Monday, July 10th Lady Barlow 'phoned that Mr John Barlow would call on me. Very glad to see him. We had a quiet Quaker talk. It was with real fervour he said: 'I am very glad you went to Germany.' I felt he understood the true inwardness of that act and I asked his advice about line of action which he promised to think over and tell me. Mr Ponsonby called also, I think, and many others but I cannot recollect all. F.W. Jowett* I think was one. He was curiously unlike what I expected and I had the same sense I always have with one-eyed people of not being able to fix on the right eye to talk into, being obsessed by the destroyed eye. I merely felt he was not greatly in sympathy with the Zimmerwald Socialists. Later Sir Wm Byles called and I took his advice about seeing Ministers. He looked very sad and aged and said he was going fast.

This afternoon too, Lord and Lady Devonport called. They came to hear about their boy Kearl[e]y whom I had seen in Ruhleben. They were simple folk and cried both of them. I liked her, though overdressed and magnificent diamonds. He, too was simple – a good worthy grocer – said he was going to make a speech in the House on the Camps and I begged him to deprecate Reprisals. This he promised to do. Asked me how to pronounce that word 'proteins'. She stayed a good while and talked on in very simple homely fashion and I gave her all the details that I could.

Tuesday, July 11th In the morning to UDC office where I met C.R. Buxton, Chas Trevelyan, E.D. Morel, J.A. Hobson, F. Pethick Lawrence, Ramsey Macdonald, Arthur Ponsonby and Mrs Swanwick. Tried to give them a sketch of Belgium and Germany and interview with von Jagow. Utterly failed to do this either with coherence, clearness or point. Realized how mentally exhausted I was and the dreadful straight-up chairs of an office tire my heart and wholly empty my brain. Made a mess of it in fact. Mrs S. left in the middle, and recollecting that she had told her Committee contrary to the promise made me, I was obliged to ask her as she left the room to keep private what she had heard. As her reply did not satisfy me I felt obliged to write to her and explain my reason for underlining this caution and after some time a stiff apology was sent. Went away feeling I had lost a great opportunity for interesting these men. At 3 p.m. Lord Loreburn came to see me. He seemed very old and shaky with a twitching head and neck – his large blue eyes still round and candid like a child's. I found him loquacious but difficult to talk to. Lord C. has warned me of this. He talked so much that I could not put in a word edgeways.

---

* Jowett was Chairman of the Independent Labour Party.

He seemed so full of his own small experiences at his home near Deal [in Kent, south-east England] which he seemed to think in the war zone! Said he and his wife stayed there to give courage to the peasantry. Continual guns of aeroplanes of both sides. Affected his dog. Very pessimistic about the future – believed universal revolution must come at the close of the war. Said government ought to negotiate and he had said so publicly and his opinions were well known but it was useless to keep nagging. Counseled me to write down all I wished to convey to Grey – in any case to write down all that von Jagow said, not what I said – and keep it – and if I desired he would hand it to Grey and see he had it. I asked him about Lord Northcliffe and if it would be well to tell him and enlist his aid. He doubted its utility but said he believed Northcliffe to be an honest man! The talk on the whole, though with points full of interest, disappointed me. Later, Mrs Buxton came to hear as much foreign news as I could give her and I delivered Elisabeth Rotten's message. Afterwards, other callers ...

Wednesday, July 12th Busy getting my pictures framed. Saw Mr Massingham at the Nation office and had a long talk with him over Ruhleben Camp – found him very sympathetic and lamenting impossibility of finding the truth. He urged me to see Northcliffe and gave me a letter to him. In his next issue he was splendid. I was relieved he promised to modify public feeling about Camps and to support principles of exchange and total exchange. Wrote and wrote ...[9]

Once again Emily had been told to write in to Foreign Office. This time it was about the needs in Belgium:

12th July 1916

Dear Lord Robert Cecil,[10]
I could have told you better than I can write but I will try to go straight to the point.

Can you, as Minister of Blockade, possibly arrange to let the Belgians have more food and let them have greater variety?

Three weeks ago I watched them being fed in Brussels and had a long talk with the Belgian who organized the Communal kitchen where they come for bread and soup. He spoke of the general enfeeblement of this section of the population which was showing itself in the development of tubercular trouble attacking the glands of the neck.

There were, he said, some 400 cases in Brussels and it was on the increase. These cases need super-alimentation, and to prevent a serious state of things all those being fed by the Comité National of Belgium need greater variety of food – such as more coffee, sugar, bacon and lard. Unfortunately the Belgians don't seem very fond of rice but they should eat more or have something which can take its place.

These people are not of the class ordinarily destitute, but respectable people who are without work owing to the war. It is true that in Brussels and to some extent in the smaller towns the German authorities have instituted works of various kinds in order to give, as they do, employment to many hundreds of women and girls, and the material for these is supplied from Germany. It remains however a sad fact that the factories where these people would for the most part be earning their livelihood are closed for want of raw material.

Would you consider letting raw material for these factories pass in like manner as the foodstuffs of the American Commission under guarantees, as then the Belgians could re-adjust their lives? I believe only their glass factories can work for which the raw material is found in the country.

I venture to ask this help for those unfortunate people because I feel sure the guarantees given by the German authorities there are faithfully kept. No food brought in by England's permission passes to Germany nor is it given to her occupying troops. I believe the head of the Political Department Baron von [der] Lancken and his colleagues Count Harrach (cousin of Lord Acton) and von Moltke to be men of the highest honour and I had to see a good deal of them.

The request I am making comes, however, from the Belgian of whom I spoke – and from my own observations in going about the country. If factory work were resumed, at least in part, it would help solve the food question as people could earn money to buy the food which the country itself produces.

I have etc. etc.

One official at the Foreign Office wrote:

This lady is a person with whom we must be very much on our guard. She acts as a German agent and there is a question of her being interned. In these circumstances I suggest that we should limit ourselves to saying politely that since we deal direct with the American Commission, her intervention is unnecessary.'[11]

So the reply came as the same flat disinterested answer from the Foreign Office. It arrived on 22 July – in a curt note addressed to 'Madam'. In fact in the Foreign Office, at the instigation of the American Commission, they had been willing to send raw materials to Belgium but said the Germans had turned down the scheme:[12]

Thursday, July 13th In the morning Emergency Camp Committee escorted thereto by Mr Rollo Russell. Astonished to find Thompson Elliot* of old Tokenbury days Chairman. Large number present and very sympathetic. Confined my remarks almost entirely to Ruhleben Camp and food in Germany. After lunch Prof. Battin** came to see me and we had a delightful talk. He brought from Holland Aletta Jacob's message – she not having fully understood the letter I had written her from Berne. I explained. Lady Lyall was to have come but did not. We agreed to meet again.

Mr Morel came about 4 p.m. and we talked about his book being now issued and he promised me a copy. He looked tired and over-worked. He asked more details that I had given at the UDC and urged also that I should write all down. Then followed Chrystal MacMillan who was very friendly and ere she left May Ellis full of sympathy as usual. Both longing to know about my talk with von Jagow in Germany, but characteristically Chrystal asked and May did not.

Friday July 14th I kept quiet in the morning preparing to talk to Lord Northcliffe at 3.30 p.m. Went to Blackfriars by bus – the old house very interesting early Georgian. As I could not do stairs, Lord Northcliffe came down very good-humouredly to see me in a long, quiet room. I sat in the window seat and he somewhat troubled by the light faced me, shading his eyes. He asked what I wanted. Then burst into a wild and unreasonable attack upon the Germans, their habits and their characters. Said he knew them well … I waited quietly till this outburst was over – it wasted some ten minutes of the interview and was like a nasty froth which had to be given off before he calmed

---

* Elliot lived not too far from the Hobhouses in Cornwall.
** Battin was an American professor, international organiser for the World Alliance for Promoting International Friendship through the Churches.

down and became quite a sane, normal man. He scanned my face intently all the time but I never moved a muscle. I think it was partly done to try what position I should take. Nevertheless, I find it a habit in most of the belligerent countries, this necessity of working off their hatred and animosity after which they become human and normal.

When sane he seemed a commonplace, good-humoured man, capable, businesslike, with a broad, low forehead and no height to his rather boyish head – means well and quite unaware there are such things as ideals. Asked how I got to Germany – said he sent two men every week and had from the beginning of the war and received back two men every week. 'Bribery,' he said, 'they are a people that will do anything for money.' I thought the man who bribes is even worse than the man who accepted it but I said nothing – merely that I went openly.

I spoke of Ruhleben and at first he said what did it matter! only 3,500 men; why, that moment he had received a wire that this number had fallen today. I said, 'Yes, but they are soldiers and go voluntarily. These are civilians trapped against their will. Those might lose life or limb, these were losing reason'. I told him of Lord Newton and the negotiations going on and the government's fear of public opinion – First making that opinion by misguidance and wrong information and then when it was excited, saying they must be guided by it. I told him I was asking the Press to keep as quiet as possible about our civilians and to restrain and modify public opinion lest the public were excited and demanded reprisals and the government would give in.

He then went off at a tangent about the Govmt, running down all the Ministers – knew them all – wretched set of fellows – would go for all of them – muddled everything.

Here the Diary ends.

Lord Northcliffe wrote to Emily from *The Times* on 17 July[13] to say that he had gone 'at once' to the American Ambassador who told him that the Germans had refused 'the very terms of exchange you mentioned to me'. As he, Northcliffe, was leaving for France the next day he said he was 'reluctantly obliged to defer further help till he got back'. He had tried to telephone her. As an afterthought he suggested she contact General Booth of the Salvation Army, which she did.

12

Ruhleben and Peace

We do not know why Emily's Diary ended abruptly on 14 July though on 16 July Emily went to see Lord Newton and will have told him about her interview with German Foreign Secretary Jagow. Lord Newton was much more sensible and amenable than the fossils who had been in the Foreign Office for years.

Newton's letter of invitation to Emily was as follows:

> 6 Belgrave Square, SW
> July 12 1916
> Private
>
> Dear Miss Hobhouse,[1]
>
> If it is any satisfaction to you, I shall be very happy to see you privately and unofficially as you suggest.
>
> If it is not inconvenient to you, perhaps, if you happen to be in London you will call here on Sunday, at any time between 10.30 and 2.
>
> Believe me, Yours very truly
> Newton

What Lord Newton thought of the story of her German visit we do not know. But to have put his upper-class Belgrave Square home at Emily's disposal, on a Sunday, his only day off, must have meant he had a sufficiently good opinion of her to make the effort. Lord Newton kept a diary but there is no indication about this meeting in it, nor what he did with the information. (From Emily's notes we know the meeting took place at 10.45 a.m.) Newton was a trained diplomat and a good public servant, so he will have passed on the information, possibly at the same time cautioning Emily to silence. Perhaps as Emily could not tell the whole tale it seemed a little unbelievable.

However, Emily knew 'how to cross her t's'. The next day she wrote:

Dear Lord Newton[2]
Thinking over our talk yesterday I rather fear one point may not have been clear.

The idea of a possible private meeting was not his but purely my own very commonplace (though I think commonsense) suggestion.

I should regret any misinterpretation about that – though I incline to think there would be no difficulty should occasion arise.

Yours very truly
E Hobhouse

In his diary, where his tiny writing is difficult to read, Lord Newton talked of the problems he was having over the camps. Ministers from the different departments attended the meetings, each with their own view which was not always relevant. It was interesting that a trickle of internees was returning from the camps all the time and each was interviewed:

July 10: Heard from Gerard [US Ambassador in Germany]. Encloses very sharp note to German Govt on refusal to allow visits and also with ref to Ruhleben.

July 12: Conference about prisoners in [?]Grey's room. R. Cecil, Curzon, [?]Walter Long, [?]Thorp, [?]Belfield, Hall etc. Inconclusive as usual. Curzon and Long knowing nothing about it, want to mix up civilians and military cases which would lead to hopeless confusion. Hall, as usual, will not consent to anyone going. Says he has about 100 submarine men, whom he cannot part with.

July 15: Visit from Pyke, who escaped from Ruhleben; seemed intelligent. Story very curious one. Six weeks military confinement, without artificial light …

July 17: Conference with five Cabinet ministers and WO [War Office] generals and Rumbold and I unable to get them to do right thing, mainly because R. Cecil had made a statement in House which would have to be contradicted. Crewe there in place of Grey.

From our point of view it is worth noting Newton's entry for 21 July, which read: 'Conv with BT [Basil Thomson, Metropolitan Police] about Miss Hobhouse. Told him I thought her quite harmless.'

No doubt disappointed at the loss of his quarry Basil Thomson recorded in his journal: 'Lord Newton thought it would not be wise to lock her up. She was a silly mischievous old* woman but not disloyal to the country.'[3]

How Thomson got from the one statement to the other is an interesting mystery! Some years later Thomson found himself in prison but that is another story.

On 19 July Arnold Rowntree, the progressive Liberal MP for York saw Cecil at the Foreign Office and got him to agree to see Emily (about the camps). Cecil said she should make arrangements with Locock.[4] Confident with this progress Emily tried to ring Locock *five times* but was unable to get through. Frustrated with 'No – Write', she sent in her scheme for the repatriation of internees with the request that it should be forwarded to Robert Cecil. Some authorities believe it never got to him but the scheme was similar to that finally adopted:

Civilian Camps In England and Germany[5]

Being that the main trouble in these camps is primarily mental, it is proposed that, in lieu of urging material reforms, camps should be abolished. Nothing is to be gained by keeping them but moral and mental decay.

There are three main categories of prisoners to be dealt with:

Those who wished repatriation

Those who merely wish release

Those of Military Age, trained and untrained.

(The problem also includes wives.)

---

* They were, in fact, much of the same age. Newton was born in 1857, Emily in 1860 and Thomson in 1862.

In considering the merits of any Scheme, numerical difference can be conveniently ignored. In the first place, the State at present holding the larger number of prisoners has the greater burden and secondly, the State that recovers the greater of its nationals will have the heavier burden of maintenance.

The scheme we would propose is:

Men of 50 and over to have the choice of:

1. repatriation taking their wives etc; or
2. internment in a Neutral State, wives remaining here as now and receiving allowances; or
3. remaining in one small selected camp with employment (say Islington) – if really Anglicised (Men who have sons fighting for us, etc.)

Men of 45–50 medically unfit to have the same privilege of choice.

All men of Military age to be interned in a Neutral State under such conditions of freedom as will permit them to follow useful occupations.

Cost. Each Government to pay the Neutral State an agreed sum per head as is done for military convalescents.

Locock told Emily he would submit her plan to Cecil. Her ideas were generally accepted but Sir Horace Rumbold said a formal letter would be sufficient response. Others agreed 'that the lady had already received enough attention',[6] – they just did not like her and possibly were afraid of her.

Dr Kaminski said the plan had been agreed in Germany. The Foreign Office thought Miss Hobhouse's scheme 'quite sensible.' But Rumbold noted the practical difficulties of finding a neutral country willing to receive prisoners, and he pointed out problems of transport and security. Moreover, Cecil commented, an alternative route of exchange through the Vatican was under consideration. (Probably it was not. He liked to be on top of everything.) Further Foreign Office officials concluded that Emily's views were doubtless 'to some extent influenced by her well-known prejudices'.[10]

On 27 July Cecil was asked in the House of Commons whether there had been any progress in the negotiations. Cecil replied that the Foreign Office was working through American Ambassador Gerard in Berlin to propose repatriation for men over 50, and those over 45 who were ill; the remaining civilian prisoners as well as merchant seamen and retired officers should be interned in a neutral country. A letter to this effect had been submitted to the Germans 'only five or six days or a week ago'. He promised that a White Paper on the correspondence would soon be published.

On 12 July Emily wrote to her brother Leonard in Manchester where he was doing summer work for the *Manchester Guardian*. He had just published his book *Questions of War and Peace*, pondering on the future of Europe. Good though it may have been, immediate peace did not enter into the equation:

Dear Leonard,[7]

The reason I wish so much to see you is not only sisterly and family in nature, but because I have recently been in Germany – Ruhleben Camp – Belgium, Berlin etc. and I thought it would be of interest and use to you and Mr Scott to hear some account thereof.

I have been and am, of course, very busy here with endless interviews etc and I do not know yet when I shall be free – the work seems to grow – and so I can't yet see my way of getting to Manchester for a talk. If you or Mr Scott ever dash up to town [London] do let me know and come and see me.

For many reasons I want this kept quiet at any rate for the present so please tell only Mr Scott.

Yrs. E H

She followed this up with a letter on 15 July:

Dear Leonard,[8]

As the possibility of getting to Manchester recedes I want at least to lose no more time in writing about Ruhleben Camp for the information of the Guardian staff.

Ruhleben is an excellent camp – as camps go (and we know they are and must be, at the best, wretched affairs) – the men have really little to complain of. I ate the bread and found it good, for myself far preferable to Italian, Swiss or Westminster Palace Hotel bread. The rations are good in quality though certainly not excessive in quantity and deficient in fats but as all Germany is on short Commons that cannot be otherwise. Every kindness possible is shown to the internees – golf, cricket, football, tennis, Theatre, Cinema, YWCA hall, Catholic and English Churches and plentiful space for exercise, Arts and Crafts, shops, Canteen, Rooms for study, books, tools etc, etc.

Graf Schwerin who till just now has been Commandant is a perfectly charming old man and beloved of all. That is universal testimony.

He gave them complete autonomy of which I regret to say I do not think they shew themselves in all respects worthy.

Compared with our Boer Camps it is a Paradise.

No – the trouble in Ruhleben is not primarily material, it is psychological and mental.

For some reason men are less able to bear inaction and loss of freedom than women (probably because we never have been free) and civilians seem far less able to bear it than prisoners of war. Various reasons account for this – they have not like soldiers had their fling and cannot take it as 'fortune of war' – they are for the most part older men and less adaptable. They are not disciplined. They have a sense of unfairness that fate caught them thus. They are worried over families and businesses etc etc.

Much more I could say on that point, but it suffices to shew why mental trouble is brewing amongst them.

The English head of the camp said we must get away the men of 45 and over – he could not pull them through another winter – they were infecting all the camp – without them the younger men might brace themselves to face it to the end. Yet I feel for them too. It is having a most unwholesome effect. Morally as well as mentally the camp is very rotten.

All this has nothing to do with the treatment shown them which is kind and good and though they get up to 40 and 45 thousand parcels a month, in all this time only one or two have gone astray. Besides the large kitchens, there is a smaller one where they can have their private food cooked to their liking.

The German Government desire and have all along desired exchange – but their story is that our Government put difficulties in their way. Here I find our Government say they wish exchange but that the Germans put difficulties.

Lord Newton however told me the Germans were right about that but Kitchener refused. On both sides I fancy the naval and military people make the trouble so Lord Newton told me.

Now I come home and from the officials and non officials alike who have worked for the Civilian Camps here, Isle of Man etc. I find exactly the same state of affairs exists. As you can imagine the Germans are equally anxious about their civilians – 28,000 – as we are about ours – 3,700.

I find also that our Government is perfectly aware of the trouble though only Lord Newton is brave enough to give it some Voice.

They know that on both sides the camps are hot beds of lunacy – yet they say 'Public Opinion' 'demands' the line they are taking viz threats. If the Public shout for Reprisals and antagonize so that no agreement for Exchange can be made it means that hundreds of these poor fellows will go out of their minds.

Now Public opinion is only shouting because it is ill informed. Ruhleben has been used as a lever to rouse feelings against Germany and no one asks for the American or other reports concerning the condition in the Isle of Man where there are 22,000 and other places.

Reprisals are beginning here in the form of excluding the workers who have brought occupation and interest and comforts into the Camps and so saved the wits of many. In Ruhleben I saw many sad cases – an artist named Brakewell, never I gather strong in the upper story, was in a pitiable condition of lost control yet he was touched by my visit and asked about you and your books which he wanted to read.

Lord Devonport, whose son I saw there, quite understood the position now and if the minds of the interned men both here and there are to be saved 'public opinion' must be calmed down and soothed – not excited with distorted and unfounded stories.

So I am begging all the Press not to defeat their own aim which is the welfare of the internees, but to guide public opinion into reasonable paths.

Retaliation and Reprisals on both sides are beginning. I am not at liberty to say how on this side – on the German side I feel sure the removal of the kind and beloved Count Schwerin is intended as a reprisal.

I have had a long talk with Mr Beaumont who was 15 months in Ruhleben and who perhaps you know. Our opinions agreed except about the bread which he did not like. There is a party of fashionable fools here who are working semi-officially and who are doing much harm. They make me tired but they mean well.

To my mind the thing to consider is the good of the civilians both in Ruhleben and the Isle of Man and that can only be attained by great calmness in dealing with the subject.

All told, Civilians and War Prisoners we have only a bare 50,000 to look after, whereas all told, Civilians and War Prisoners, Germany has over 2 million to look after and is a blockaded country to boot.

I have much to tell you about Belgium but cannot now – I suppose you saw the official denial from Brussels to yr. attack?

Yrs in haste

E. Hobhouse

Continually interrupted while writing this.

So the correspondence went on. On 17 July Leonard wrote:[9]

I am interested in your account of Ruhleben. It is always worth while collecting impressions … [He had seen a man just back from the camp whose view was not so rosy as hers] … But I think even women would get on one another's nerves and would probably do so if living for two years six in a horse box, unable to go in or out without making every-one sit up …

He apparently thought Emily was producing a prejudiced picture. It will be noted she hadn't mentioned the accommodation at all. Why? It was not likely, though possible in the circumstances, to have been an oversight. It is more probable that she knew it was potential dynamite and did not want to detract from her message. It was a miscalculation that was to cost her.

She replied 23 July:[10]

…I quite agree six in a horse box for two years is trying – but if the Boer women had had such good accommodation they would not have died – as Ruhleben men don't die. 14–16 in a Bell tent then mostly sleeping on the earth is as your informant would find a bit worse …

[She had read the reports and did not defend any tyrannies (An appalling report was shortly to come out about Wittenberg camp which Emily passed on her journey through Germany. It was written by the English doctors, one of whom contracted typhus. Certainly the Germans were not always good organisers!] …

Yes– indeed I have had a time of extraordinary interest and now am hard at work about these Camps. With the help of Press and some MPs I hope extinction of the Camps may be attained – broadly repatriation of the old men and Internment in a neutral state of those of Military age. I have drawn up the scheme for Lord Robert – but that is the broad basis. I hope it may succeed but it will probably cost me getting to Bude. Still no one deserves holidays.

Yrs EH

Anyhow work for that idea – then the Govt will call it 'public opinion' and be led by it.

On 25 July Leonard wrote:[11]

… don't let us get into controversy, but you go your side of the street and I go mine. We both agree that the thing to do is to get the prisoners exchanged if possible, and, if not, to resist reprisals …

[He asked what she was going to do about a holiday at Bude.] We go there on 11th' [August] … [Both his daughters were doing hospital work in Wimbledon, and tragically his wife's nephew, Noel Hadwen, had been killed in the attack on 1 July.] … a good sort, and a promising career gone …

Emily had now submitted or proposed two articles to the *Manchester Guardian*, one on Ruhleben and one on Belgium and they had both been dismissed. Possibly the newspaper had been warned Emily might be subscribing to the German point of view.

It must have been a bitter disappointment to Emily, as she had expected the paper would respond positively. Her answer to Leonard on 2 August is quite bitter:

No dear Leonard[12] – I did not in the least mind the refusal of my article – on the contrary I expected it … I am perfectly aware the Press today prefers to obscure the truth …

No I did not answer all your arguments about Ruhleben, nor fully, any – because controversy bores me and I have no time for it. I now enclose the general basis Scheme which we are working through. Practically all the London Press has promised me to support it and the Archbishop also – and others of sundry kinds.

So if the Press keeps its head at all there is a chance of success.

13

AUGUST 1916 — CLOAK AND DAGGER

Emily had been working on a new idea. On 2 August 1916, she arranged to meet with Randall Davidson, Archbishop of Canterbury. Randall Davidson was known to be interested in Ruhleben, and Emily hoped he would help not only with the exchange of internees but especially with starting peace talks. In her notes he described him and her visit:[1]

Friendly — kind eyes — well meaning. A small man rattling about in a big place; unable to fill it but wanting to do his duty. Listened about Ruhleben, said he was of my opinion — viz inclined to believe that Ruhleben was not so bad as painted and ours not so good as painted. Acknowledged that the Press had recently shown restraint. Had already spoken against Retaliation. Saw my point that apart from being unXtian [unChristian] and inhuman it was a fatal policy for our men. Took a long time telling me how he had been caricatured as 'pro-Kaiser' for his speeches against Reprisals. Feared to be thought nagging if repeated his views too often.

Promised to do what he could. Would see Lord Newton. I begged for strong utterance to give the leading note. If the tide of Militarism was rising as it seems, at least the Xtian [Christian] church should say 'This cannot be tolerated; thus far and no further.'

Later we passed to speak of my interview with von Jagow. He refused to believe that Alsace-Lorraine had been offered to the French. I told him I knew it not from von Jagow's lips but from two high authorities but I told him what von J had conveyed to me, his general attitude of moderation and reason ... I spoke of the right hand of fellowship held out by Germany if we would take it. I went further and told him, and him only, of that which I had promised von Jagow. He said that the fact I had put the seal on his lips, nullified its importance; no step could be advanced.

Said a thing told Confidentially was of no use unless told to the person responsible. I said that the knowledge would, I hoped, have strengthened any effort he could make. He said, 'No; it would not'. Rather urged me to reconsider if I could conscientiously relax my promise in any degree. Said the letters I left behind were of great importance. [In Switzerland perhaps, – there is no indication as to what these letters were unless they were the correspondence with von Jagow.] Spoke at length on this point and repeated himself a good deal. Wished me to be clear that nothing advanced without my permission to unseal his lips.

As Emily came away from the meeting she realised she had to get a message to Jagow to ask him to release her from her promise. Her promise was not to divulge that he was willing to talk peace (on the grounds that Britain could take it as a sign of weakness). She will have considered her options, and, although nothing is written, I believe decided that the best approach would be through the German section at the American Embassy. To go through her contacts in Switzerland or the Netherlands would take too long.

By a letter[2] we know she went to the German section of the Embassy and was well received. We can only surmise that she was able to arrange for a message to be sent either to the German Minister in Switzerland, Baron von Romberg, or to Jagow himself.

What neither she nor the Embassy knew was that as all cables passed through British hands messages could be intercepted, and the name Miss Hobhouse would have raised a red flag. That this happened could explain Cecil's unexpected statements in the House of Commons both on the exchange of internees and the acceptable procedure for starting peace talks.

The thought of her Embassy visit could also account for his virulent attacks on Emily herself in October. The Foreign Office did not appreciate interference from *anyone*.

While Emily was at the Embassy the suggestion was probably made that she write to the US Ambassador, Dr Walter Hines Page, with a request that the President intervene in the process of getting the internees repatriated. She wrote a good and sincere letter but we know that this move may not have been entirely necessary at that time, so it could have been partly as a 'cover' for her visit. If news of this letter got back to the Foreign Office they would not have cared for that either.

She wrote: [3]

August 5th 1916

Yr Excellency,

Will you allow me, on the broad basis of humanity, to write to you quite privately and unofficially and even without introduction?

It has been suggested to me in the course of my work for the release of Civilian Prisoners in the camps of England and Germany, and even urged by various prominent persons, that the President of the United States is the one Personage who could take the matter up with success and by appealing simultaneously to the two Governments bring them into agreement by a promise to himself.

As the President is beyond our reach. I was counselled to ask your Excellency if you would in private capacity or not as seems to you best, bring this request before him …

[She proceeded to outline what she hoped could happen.]

Indeed the moment seems ripe for such action – Salvation in lieu of Destruction, a refreshing thought and the whole question would thus be lifted to a higher plane and like the Red Cross removed from the Spirit of War. About 35,000 men are concerned; and this seems but a small number in contrast with the vast figures of the Military, but their fate affects also thousands of women and children – their wives and families …

Should apology be needed for this appeal I hope and believe you will grant it when I tell you that I solemnly promised the men at Ruhleben and the German Government to leave no stone unturned to obtain the release of both sets of prisoners.

The United States was not yet at war with Germany. Like many peace activists Emily had great faith in the abilities of the Americans to take a dispassionate view and help in the international field.

On 9 August 1916 she wrote to the Archbishop of Canterbury the confidential draft of which read:[4]

Your Grace,

I have thought long and seriously but cannot feel I should do right to relax my promise on the point we discussed. At any rate not at present. Opportunity is offering itself by which to ask if the prohibition can be removed.

I pray it may be, for words fail to express how strongly I feel that we are all wrong to continue this slaughter, and as in the end Negotiation must be resorted to. How desirable – nay how urgent to begin at once.

All that your Grace pointed out to me was exceedingly helpful and I am very grateful for it; nevertheless I cannot abandon my belief that the knowledge of a fact bearing written [in] it such a disposition of goodwill and readiness on the other side cannot fail to be an inward strength to anyone placed in a position to plead with the Government and to lead the Nation in the highest paths. It may lack legal importance apart from full disclosure but does it not contain spiritual value of greater import?

Your Grace – I have mixed these two years with the peoples of Holland, Italy, Switzerland, Germany, France and Belgium – besides our own country, and everywhere the same 'darkness covers the earth and thick darkness the people.'

All alike grope for the Light to arise and shine and there is but one Light to illumine Humanity – the Love Eternal which comprehends and embraces all nations alike.

I am jealous for our Country that she should be the exponent of this Love that she should initiate a great moral and spiritual act such as would make her 'blessed amongst nations'. Without this it seems to me that our righteousness is as rags.

My hope in telling you what I did was just this – that the knowledge that our opponent would support and forward such effort would give irresistible power – and multitudes at home and abroad would rise up and call you blessed.

If I presume on pressing this point I beg your Grace to pardon me — realizing that it is the outcome of a passionate desire not merely to hasten Peace but still more — see it attained by the power of the Spirit rather than by the murderous Powers now at work.

I have the honour to be

Yrs obediently

Emily Hobhouse

In a PS she said she had heard from Lord Beauchamp (a former Cabinet Minister) to whom she had spoken to about the Civilian Camps that he would be glad to assist the Archbishop in any way over the question of internees.

At the parliamentary session on 10 August, Commander Wedgewood commented to Cecil in the House of Commons that the British people wished 'to get rid of' the more than 20,000 Germans interned in Britain in exchange for the 4,000 British in Germany. Cecil answered that negotiations were stuck on the issue of numbers, as Britain wished to keep the exchange of men of military age equal. This stand was supported by Grey stressing military considerations.

However, the previous day, 9 August, Lord Newton had written to Emily:[5] 'We are negotiating with the German Gov. for the exchange of civilians. If this should happily be effected or if they were interned in neutral countries, then camps here would naturally cease to exist.'

Emily noted on the back of her press cutting: 'The exchange question seems to be going along satisfactorily so I'd better not include that in the message.' This would seem to refer to her reply to Lord Newton's letter. She was not fooled by Cecil's remarks, which may however have annoyed Newton, who was dealing with the sensitive negotiations.

While at the American Embassy Emily would have talked about Belgium. A few days later she had a letter from Herbert Hoover, the future US President, who was running the Belgian food programme.[6] Unlike the Foreign Office officials Hoover was anxious to see her, and as he passed her hotel each evening, offered to visit her there on any evening *convenient to her.* (Notes of that interview follow later, and the letter appears as Plate 6.)

Emily's first published article was on the Leader page of the *Daily News*, 8 August 1916. It was published anonymously and was entitled 'Life in Germany — from a correspondent'. It was introduced as follows:

The writer passed through Germany within the last few weeks. The record, which does not agree with the evidence generally received as to the internal condition of Germany, is offered only as a personal impression.

The aspect of Germany is so different from the picture usually painted, that it was almost a shock to see the tranquil condition of the country and the calm confidence of the people. The wide plains were waving with corn, promising well up to that midsummer moment – the harvest upon which so much depends for the coming year. Everywhere haymaking was proceeding apace with what looked like a heavy crop. Down the Rhine Valley the cherries were ripening, and men and women (chiefly women) were climbing the trees and gathering the fruit. Later one saw the barrows in Berlin piled with these cherries, and heard that the stones of all fruit were to be saved and collected this year and the kernels crushed for oil. This economical form of natural housekeeping has great attractions for the frugal mind, and one wonders why one needs a war to prevent waste and inculcate economy.

A beautiful sight it was in the long midsummer evenings to see a Zeppelin sailing aloft … Surely Zeppelins will shortly be vehicles possessed by all for sky trips, opening new worlds, a precious means of closer intercommunication safeguarded by Hague Rules from evil-practices.

Share and Share Alike

Germany is living very carefully in these days, the strain falling heaviest during these final weeks before the harvest is gathered; then the national larder will be better filled. The blockade policy has certainly caused privation, and privation spells suffering for many innocent people; but not of a nature or magnitude to influence the war. Indeed the Social Democrats assert that had the distribution of food been taken in hand earlier, and luxurious waste prohibited at first, there need have been no scarcity today. Their scheme of food distribution submitted to the Government over a year ago was at the time disregarded, now it is recognized as a necessity and point by point is being adopted. What a marvellous leveller this must prove, when in matters of food all must share and share alike. The rich it is true can obtain variety by the purchase of luxuries, but necessaries are now being strictly regulated for the good of all. A man may not have a pound of butter and his neighbour none, each must have four ounces (now further reduced to three ounces a week) and must make that serve for table and cooking. The housewife is learning, she says, to cook as the English do, namely to grill steaks and chops, and in all things to return to the simpler habits which satisfied the country before 1870.

Every day, they say, they are learning some new method. Soon, too, when the hay is saved and the crops garnered, the cows can be turned into the fields to fatten and yield more milk. That at least is their hope. Meantime their war bread, the 'K Bread' which has been so much decried, is very excellent and wholesome and being less dry than much Continental bread it is easy to eat without butter. Fish is abundant. At the restaurants ordinary food was not dearer than in other countries, but luxuries were high. Portions were perhaps smaller but that was less noticeable in Berlin than in Cologne where they were extremely small. At a large working women's restaurant under philanthropic management the food was very well prepared, excellent in quality and quantity, and provided for 3d per head.

The Food Queues

The habit of standing in queues outside the shops now almost universal, to get their share of meat or groceries is very trying for the women. They feel the waste of time and get restless and impatient, with the result that several miniature street riots have arisen; these are not, however, considered of any importance.

Up to the present the general population does not seem to have been very seriously affected in health and the anticipated improvement in distribution and supply will relieve the severity of the pressure felt by the poor. Infants under 1 year and children aged from 10–14 have hitherto been the chief sufferers. A doctor of the municipal schools stated that he had weighed all the school children of Berlin last year and again this year finding no divergence from the normal but he admitted a general enfeeblement of children of the ages above named. Figures show that children of those ages living in the large towns have died to the number of 5,000 above the normal during the past twelve months of blockade but in the country districts no increase has been observed.

A well-known clergyman who inhabited the poorer quarters of Berlin and who lives as the poor there live acknowledged very simply: 'We are hungry, we are often very hungry; but we do not mind.'

This article had to be submitted to the censor and was cut. Emily had said, in effect, that applying the blockade did not improve the feeling towards the British.

The same day, 8 August, Dr Markel wrote to her from the Prisoners of War Relief Agency enclosing a cutting that said Emily had been to Ruhleben.[7] 'So,' he said, 'it seems your visit to Ruhleben is a secret no more.' He also said that he was not allowed to visit the camps any more* and this only increased his work, 'as also of course the large influx of fresh prisoners, especially wounded'. He hoped to see her very soon.

Emily had at last managed to get to Bude, but was prepared to come up to London for meetings. In Bude there was a family gathering. Leonard, Nora and their girls were there; Leonard Courtney and his wife Kate; and Kate's sister Maggie (Margaret), who was married to their cousin Henry.

Maggie Hobhouse was much concerned about her eldest son, Stephen, the Quaker convert, who was absolutely opposed to conscription for the army which was now in force. He was determined not to do ambulance work or any other work to take the easy way out. He was prepared to go to prison, which he later did. He was not a strong man and his mother was at this point trying to do all she could to keep him out of jail. What with Emily's efforts, Leonard told Oliver, who was with the army in Burma, they could expect a lot of notoriety.[8]

Oliver's reaction was interesting.[9] While he was being ribbed about Emily and thought he would have to wear a placard saying: 'Yes, my Aunt', he said he had no patience at all with Stephen. He said: 'We have buried our souls and are prepared to put our bodies on the line.' He must have talked for many of his contemporaries. Religion had lost its hold. For a thousand years, at a time when people were expected, even compelled, to go to church, the message of peace had been proclaimed from the pulpit but it had not been acted on. The message had failed to go deep enough.

On 15 August Emily received an obscure telegram from Gertrud Woker in Switzerland, via Leonard Courtney, that she should be at the St Ermin's Hotel [Westminster, London] on the next day.[10] She will have been overjoyed to hear of her friend, and possibly this provided her with the opportunity she needed to get a message through to German Foreign Minister von Jagow to ask if she could be released from her promise.

---

* Possibly a reprisal.

She prepared a postcard on 16 August for Dr Kocher in Berne to give to the German Ambassador, Romberg.[11] It read:

> Have you seen anything of Henry or has he also gone away for his holiday? If he would ask his Chief to release me from the promise I made I think something might be done pretty soon. Do try and see him and tell him so …
>
> Anyhow the door was not shut in my face rather postponement suggested and I am not entirely dissatisfied considering the moment was not opportune.

It seems Emily had not receved a reply from von Jagow at the German Foreign Office.

We now pass to a new venture. One of the leaders of the women's movement in Denmark, Henni Forchhammer, was a fluent English speaker who later became the first woman to speak at the League of Nations. She was in England with a party of delegates. They were interested in civilian detainees and in peace. Although Henni's group did not have any success in seeing government members, she met Emily at the St Ermin's Hotel and they struck up an immediate rapport. Henni told Emily:

> I am so happy that I've made your acquaintance and hope that the time may not be far away when we can meet under more peaceful conditions. Till then we must not lay down our weapons fighting for the best cause in the world. It has been such a help and inspiration for me to meet you …

They again agreed on a code so a message could be got to von Jagow. This time he was Jack![12]

Here Emily kept a few pages of Notes.[13] She was working hard and thriving on it:

Aug 15: Came to London – saw Miss Forchhammer supped together – She told me all her mission.
Aug 16: Went early to St Ermins to tell Miss Forchhammer she should try to see Archbishop – told her of my interview and correspondence with him and suggested that hers would endorse and verify what I had said. She agreed.

Went to UDC and saw Mr Buxton. Spoke to him of Negotiation work – and how to arrange meetings and speakers. He alluded to lack of money.

At 3 p.m. Dr. Markel called and we had a two hour talk. He spoke of our work for Civilian Camps. Of Dr. Taylor's Confession of Error – of Donnington Hall, of tiresomeness of the American Embassy, of the need of Peace. Wished to forward the Negotiations Memorial and offered me money up to £100 or £200 to organize meetings. Great faith in Dunnico [Secretary of the Peace Negotiations Committee of which Emily was a member].

After him came Mr Outhwaite to bring White Book and we chatted. Said that in this offensive (six weeks) 300,000 men and 10,000 officers were the casualties [still the Battle of the Somme].

Mr Hoover came and I dismissed Mr Outhwaite and went to receive him. Very nice – talked facts for one and a half hours a great strain on my ears and brain. Very clear and neutral.[14] Advised that I, an English woman, should write to help Belgium something to arouse the English Conscience. Left Reports …

Said peasantry better off – good harvest and fruit and veg – high prices. Said babies up to 3 yrs better and mortality reduced for well looked after. Said rich classes in good trim for various reasons. Burden falling on 5 millions of intermediate 'petite bourgeoisie', and artizans [sic] and factory hands – especially on children from 5–16 and age of adolescence.

Confirmed what I had learned –Vital Statistics carefully tabulated tubercular trouble 600 per cent above normal.

They are now spending 1.6 million a month and only the 1 million is from the Belgian Government. Fears he won't be able to maintain the rest more than two or three months.

Can't get Allied Govts to let in more fats – need 10,000 tons a month, only allowed about 2,500 but hopes 3,200 next month. Has arranged at cost of £200,000 a month to give meals to school children in all the towns a good midday meal. Wants Sanatorium for tuberculosis – will try Rockefeller.

Said Germans kept letter of law often broke spirit – took fish of artificial ponds, took wool but left sheep – took half sugar produced at 35 cy (only 60,000) and sold in Germany for 3 frs. Left Belgium with half supply but this not under guarantee at the time.

No Belgian would work on the railways. Out of 80,000 employ-
ees to whom the Belgian Govent sent 30 frs a week thro' the Relief,
only 250 would work for the Germans. Co-erced Labour not success.
About five men a week shot in Brussels for Espionage technically
correct because treason.

Spoke well of Captain Bruhn, a fine man. And well, but not so well,
of von Lancken etc. Visé and Tirlmin quite destroyed. 800,000 cattle
left in Belgium.

157 districts to which Relief Commission distribute supplies and
then leave to Belgians. This necessary as they are not always fair to
each other. People get 60 per cent of minimum necessity.

Spoke of difficulties with Belgian Government. Grey and Cecil
humane — Kitchener impossible. Better now with Lloyd George.

Hard to find ships. Scrape up anywhere. Enormous prices for voyage
to Rotterdam worst there is. Pay the cost of the vessel in two trips.
Not ships enough and much much more. Feed on the basis of 5 frs per
capita [a week?]. Had all the cereal harvest last year and again this …'

When Theodor Kocher received Emily's message, 23 August, he answered
with an eye to the censor:[15]

Today I got your message. We were so glad, my wife and I — as we
had not heard from you such a long time. We found it very hot here
in coming back from the mountains ten days ago. I did not hear from
Henry since our return. But still I can not think he would have been
able to go away being hard at work. I shall try and see him tomorrow.
This would be a very fine scheme to go to your sea altogether. I hope
your stay shall give you much benefit. I am happy to think you are not
absolutely disappointed and send best wishes, which my wife joins. She
sends her love to you. The holidays did much good to the children.
     Yours T K.

Dr Kocher sent a little formal note off via Romberg to Jagow in the
German Foreign Office [undated on file]:[16]

Miss Emily Hobhouse says: The moment was inauspicious but the
door was not entirely shut in her face. The matter was rather postponed awhile.

She asks: Is it possible to withdraw the prohibition made by Hr v. J. in writing and release her promise to respect it. If so she has reason to believe that something may be done very soon.

Sadly, for Emily the answer was '*Nein*' [No].[17] In the German Foreign Office they were probably well aware of the difficulties Emily was having.

And there was another disappointment. If Emily thought she had made some headway with Tom Newton her doubts were raised once again on 23 August when in answer to a question in the House from Sir Henry Dalziel, Liberal MP for Kilcaldy Burghs, Cecil said:

In the first place the Rt Hon. gentleman asked me whether any overtures for peace had been made to the British Government. I can say quite definitely and explicitly that no such overtures have been made. There is only one way in which overtures of peace can be made and that is by communication of the enemy governments to this Government. If any such communication had taken place the first thing we would have had to do would be to consult our Allies. No such overture has taken place of any kind …

Emily wrote hurriedly to Tom Newton:

Draft Confidential
Aug 24/16

Dear Lord Newton,[18]

When I read Lord Robert's reply to Sir H Dalziel in the Times today I felt very uncomfortable.

I feel so sure that what von Jagow said to me was an indirect overture for peace but perhaps in my blundering way I did not make it clear to you. He said that as Germany has (and she believes she has) made two open pronouncements of her desire for peace and her readiness to enter into negotiations to arrange it – and has received only insults in reply (for this is her view) – therefore it is impossible for her to make another public move, it must come from our side now, but on the other hand she is ready and more than ready and desirous for peace – and, it is obvious would be very moderate in her terms.

Also he expressly answered Viscount Grey's remark when he said the first step towards peace would be when Germany recognized and acknowledged that the Allies are not beaten – von Jagow said that 'they fully recognized that England was not defeated.'

It seems to me so horrible this massacre and misery when all the time the right hand of fellowship is ready for our grasp.

If only you could meet him privately I feel more and more sure you would together find a basis for public negotiation.

Forgive me for writing this but it is prompted by a feeling of responsibility as if I had not clearly conveyed what I believe undoubtedly was an indirect word of great import as regards their willingness.

Newton answered privately 27 August: 'I think you must realise that, in view of my holding an official position, it is quite impossible for me to act as you suggest.'[19]

To return to Ruhleben. Lord Newton recorded in his diary: 'August 15: Hear that Asquith is in favour of letting all German civilians go, personally, and that Robertson [Army] is difficulty.'

In the following week Newton had interviews with both Asquith and Grey, Asquith claiming he knew nothing about the subject but was quite surprised to hear there was any opposition: 'seemed sensible enough and in favour of it.'

Grey also promised support to let all prisoners over the age of 45 go free. Newton had pointed out that this was the only chance of getting anything done and noted in his diary that it remained to be seen if he, Grey, would 'stick to it'.

About two months later Lord Newton gained complete control of his Prisoners of War Department. In the House of Lords he said he was of a very conciliatory nature and would like to send home all civilians over military age, who wanted to go.

On 15 November the Archbishop of Canterbury asked in the Lords what progress had been made in the exchange of civilian prisoners, and Lord Devonport talked of the numbers to be exchanged. He said he understood it had been agreed in Germany on an all-for-all basis – with the proviso that those of military age would not be permitted to serve in the army or navy.[20]

The question of numbers – whether it was for those over military age, 400 British for 6,000 Germans, or all for all, about 4,000 British for about 26,000 of the enemy – must have provided a moral dilemma for the government, over and above objections from the military. It is to the credit of the Government, to Lord Newton and to Emily, that the needs of humanity were chosen over those of fair play. Emily had done what she could.

The question of the actual exchange was to linger on.

14

BELGIUM, PEACE AND THE PUSH BACK

Emily wrote to Isabella Steyn on 3 September.[1]

> We pacifists dare not pause – far less than those who make destructive munitions of war ... Fancy our beloved country, fancy France, fancy beautiful Italy and Germany, all given up to making death-dealing instruments, girls and boys hard at it night and day* in all our countries. It is ghastly, and 28 millions of men hurling these things at each other, each seeing who can kill the most ... You have no idea of the state of affairs.

She said Leonard Courtney had taken a house near her (in Bude) and they talked daily. And she told Isabella, in confidence, that she had been to Belgium and Germany.

On 28 August Arthur Ponsonby had sent Emily the depressing news that he did not think she could do anything further:

> They won't listen. They don't want to hear of any approaches. They are determined to ignore any indirect overtures because they are

---

* In England, munitions workers had to give up their August bank holiday.

under the impression that in time they will be able to force Germany
into submission. What is worse is that they [meaning the Foreign
Office] haven't an idea of what they want or how these huge problems
are to be solved and what sort of settlement is going to leave Europe
in a better condition in the future. Nothing you can say to Grey or
anyone else will alter this state of mind. But in the Autumn I trust
we shall be able to speak out. At present it is very desperate and one's
incompetence in the face of such a hideous calamity is sometimes
almost unbearable.[2]

'Haven't an idea ...' Unfortunately, looking at just a small portion of the
Foreign Office files this seems to be the situation. A plaintive remark
I found somewhere said: 'It is Mesopotamia we are fighting about isn't it',
which suggests there was no direct policy. Asquith did canvas for opinions
in the autumn of 1916. Most seemed to favour Lloyd George's 'knock-out
blow' though they had no idea how they were going to get it.

The opinion of the ordinary man and woman was not canvassed: the
fighting spirit, and a feeling of optimism fanned by the press, prevailed.

As we will see, Emily had ideas and was busy.

Arthur Ponsonby, Leonard Courtney and Ramsay Macdonald, were prominent members of the Peace Negotiation Committee of which Emily was
also a member. Members were speaking up and down the country hoping
to gain support. In August Emily was able to get 5,000 leaflets printed
for them from an unidentified source – probably K.E. Markel who said,
at the time, he would prefer to remain anonymous but, if it would help,
would let his name be known.[3] (If he was responsible, the money may
have come from German sources, a matter which would have interested
Scotland Yard.)

Besides this, always thorough, Emily had been round to see the Honorary
Secretary of the National Committee for Relief in Belgium and had had
his blessing on the article she was contemplating entitled 'In Belgium'.[4]
This 3,000-word article was published under her name in *UDC*, the
Union of Democratic Control paper, and Sylvia Pankhurst's *The Woman's
Dreadnought*.[5] It was also picked up by *The* [London] *Herald*. Emily wanted
to be sure what was published was what she had written and that the
meaning was not lost in the editing. A typed copy of this article, sent from
the Union of Democratic Control reached the German Foreign Office in

Berlin and was circulated. In it, it was stated that the article was written at the request of the UDC.[6]

However, Emily told C.E. Maurice, the Honorary Secretary of her old South African Women and Children Distress Fund: 'It was written at the express desire of the American Commission and the English Belgium Relief Fund and was not intended to ask for private charity – but to call public attention to the very serious outbreak of tuberculosis in Belgium' – which in fact this particular article does not mention.[7]

The article chronicled at length the structural damage done to the towns Emily visited. As the damage was considerably less than that generally reported in the press, this could have been comforting to some of the many refugees in Britain, which was her intention. She blamed food shortages on the blockade and felt that, when the war ended, the Germans would leave Belgium with more thankfulness than the Belgians 'who watch them go'.

She said she hoped her observations would bring exaggerated stories of destruction into perspective and also convince the people of the futility of war.

She also said that she felt Belgium had escaped fairly well from the 'talons' of war compared with South Africa in the Anglo-Boer War, where 30,000 farms had been burnt, to say nothing of towns and villages razed to the ground. (The policy in South Africa was to destroy the farm houses so that food and shelter would not be available to the Afrikaner farmers conducting a guerilla war. Farm burning started early in 1901 and continued to war's end in May 1902 whereas the damage in Belgium was done over a comparatively short period in 1914.)

She said that 'if only for the sake of the Belgians' she wished peace could be negotiated to protect the country from further destruction 'through air raids'. For she said that, 'since writing, a *Reuters* telegram published in *The Times*, 29 September, said that during a recent bombing raid on Brussels, fifteen houses were destroyed, thirteen Belgians killed and twenty-eight injured.' (The object of this air raid was unexplained.)

Emily's references to bombing, and to South Africa, must have made for uncomfortable reading. People thought, erroneously, that she had been deliberately shown only the undamaged parts of the towns she visited. Those wiser, but still distrusting her, commented that her accounts could not be verified until the end of the war. For *The Herald* it provided another reason for negotiated peace 'to save Belgium from the utter destruction which would inevitably ensue from the clash of huge contending armies on her soil'.[8]

For us who stand outside events and are living 100 years later, one can be sad that in the article Emily did not discuss the psychological problems for people living under German rule – even in so far as she was able to observe them. In this she missed an opportunity for service, for it has been suggested that if these problems had been better known and understood there would have been a better informed opposition and protest to Adolf Hitler's acquisitions in the 1930s.[9]

She also did not feel able to give an account of the restrictions under which she was placed – especially that she was forbidden to talk to the non-combatants – and though she said the fact that she saw Belgians and German soldiers kneeling side by side in prayer gave her the hope that 'the possibility of universal brotherhood still lives', she made herself open to being called pro-German, and as a result what she wrote was called into question.

One concludes that one of her objects was to placate the 'war party' in England. This is important but unfortunately her article may not have reached the right people.

On 15 October Lord Newton wrote from home:[10]

I have only this evening returned from a visit to France, and do not know yet whether any fresh developments have taken place, but as we have offered about 7,000 Germans in exchange for about 600 British civilians, we can scarcely be charged with driving a hard bargain.

Nearly two years later, in July 1918, while Newton was in Holland still trying to get prisoners exchanged, it came to his attention that the Germans 'were acutely, almost passionately anxious to enter upon peace negotiations'.[11] He was very surprised as the Germans seemed well entrenched in France and were causing enormous damage at sea. He said 'it was intimated [to him] that they were willing to evacuate Belgium and to pay an indemnity and that there was no intention of retaining territory in Alsace and Lorraine,' thus supporting what Emily had said when she returned from Germany.

E.D. Morel of the Union of Democratic Control wrote to Emily on 16 October 1916 asking her to convey to her good friend Signora Chiaraviglio, the daughter of the former Italian Prime Minister Giovani Giolitti, his thanks for all she was doing for UDC.[12] He was immensely impressed as well as personally glad that Chiaraviglio was now translating his book *Truth and the War* into Italian. He enclosed various leaflets for Emily to send on. As we have observed, the wheels of government work slowly and about ten months later Morel was arrested and imprisoned for six months on a similar case where he sent leaflets abroad.[13] We do not know if Morel's correspondence with Emily was intercepted but Emily and her friends had a poor view of the censorship arrangements and were not apparently overly worried if they avoided the censor to get their point of view across.

Emily had a letter published in *The Times*, 18 October which was a comment on its article on Louvain of 3 October:

> In it, you mention the 'destruction of Louvain' … During my recent visit to see our civilians in Ruhleben and our non-combatant Belgian friends, I spent a day in Louvain and was somewhat astounded to find that, contrary to Press assertions, it is not destroyed. Indeed, out of a normal population of 44,000, 38,000 are living there today. It is computed that only an eighth part of the town suffered. The exquisite town hall is unscathed, the roof of the cathedral caught fire, the bells melting and crashing into the nave, but the flames were extinguished before too great damage was done to the main structure … The library is, of course, a sad sight, for in spite of great efforts, only the walls remain …

The Times answered immediately:

> The truth about Louvain will be known as soon as the German lines are no longer in front of it, when it will be possible to visit it without receiving privileges from the enemy. In the meantime, on the evidence before us, we maintain the accuracy of the sentence which Miss Hobhouse quotes. No one imagines that Louvain was destroyed in the sense that the 'Cities of the Plain' [Biblical] were destroyed: and according to the Bryce report, 'the burning of a large part of Louvain' was 'due to a calculated policy carried out scientifically and deliberately' and according to the Belgian Commission of Inquiry which said the greater part of the town was prey to the flames. The fire burnt for several days. Further the writer said the rumour that some of the books had been removed has been disposed of.*

---

* Under the 1919 Treaty of Versailles (part VIII, section II) Germany was required to supply the university with articles of similar value to those destroyed.

A fierce argument ensued for not only had Emily taken on Britain's most influential paper but indirectly the whole propaganda machine.

Correspondence reflected the anger and distress of those who had lost their homes and livelihood.[14] People were unshaken in their belief that the fires had been deliberately set and talked of the shooting of hostages – about which Emily knew, but had not mentioned in her articles. The number of hostages shot may also have been higher than Emily was led to believe.

Emily replied she had read most of the 'excellent authorities cited':

It is so bad to have the eighth part of your town destroyed and the eighth part of its inhabitants homeless, that only intense relief can result from learning that seven–eighths are left in tranquility. I use, of course, approximate figures.

Far greater to my mind than the material havoc in the town and elsewhere in Belgium is the underfed condition of the industrial section of the community – some 5 million. These people are suffering in large numbers from a most serious outbreak of tuberculosis. The wonderful work of Mr Hoover and the Belgium Relief Committee has hitherto preserved them, but their needs are pressing, winter confronts us, and I would earnestly beg all who can to send money and clothing to help the sufferers in this special need.

I am etc …[15]

The British Foreign Office now realised it would soon have to deal with the subject of Miss Hobhouse in Parliament. It hastily opened a file and reviewed all it had done. It knew it had treated her shabbily, that in spite of her continued requests it had not seen her. But once again Emily was badly served. The Foreign Office Library, which was asked for a profile, only said she was the niece of Lord Hobhouse, had gone to South Africa (in the Anglo-Boer War) to distribute relief to the camps and when she went out again was sent home. No mention was made of her recommendations or of her campaign to get improvements in the camps and so save lives, nor of her efforts up and down the country to arouse public opinion which led in turn to the formation of a Ladies Commission who supported her findings. No one in the Foreign Office appears to have corrected, the omission although it was well known.[16]

Here we should note that different Government departments were involved in 1901–02, then the War Office, in 1916 the Foreign Office. The Foreign Office was not involved in 1901–02, rather the Colonial Office.

No doubt Foreign Office officials wondered how to defend their position, and found that when Emily said she was going to Italy for her health, she was also carrying out peace propaganda, and that when she said she was going to Holland to stay with friends she was also working for permanent peace. In both cases what she said was true and unless she was specifically asked for more information surely it could not be expected that she would give it.

At last Emily was prepared to publish a report of her interview with German Foreign Secretary, Gottlieb von Jagow. Leonard Courtney's biography says that Courtney had listened to Emily's description of the interview 'with eager interest' and had advised her to publish it after affording Grey an opportunity to veto the publication if he desired.[17] Emily was prepared to give the government this one last chance. She wrote via the Archbishop of Canterbury who thought his best course of action would be to send Emily's letter with its enclosure privately to Viscount Grey so that he could get in touch with her if he thought it desirable.[18] Presumably this was done but there is no record in the Foreign Office files.

At the same time Emily wrote to the Archbishop on 10 October: 'The point mentioned to you in confidence which I am under promise not to make known is *still reserved*.'[19] We do not know if she received Jagow's pencilled message of '*Nein*' in answer to her request to be released from her promise, but she was prepared to go as far as she could without betraying his confidence.[20] Theodor Kocher had written again to Romberg on 13 September: 'Yesterday evening I received again a postcard with the remark: "I look forward with impatience to hear from you if I can be released from my promise as I think good would result from such a course." I wanted to inform you about this.'[21]

When Emily received no response from either Foreign Office she authorised *The Nation* to publish the following letter. It was published 21 October under the title:

'A German official's view of Peace'
Sir,

During my visit to Germany this summer, where I journeyed in the interests of our fellow-countrymen in Ruhleben Camp, opportunity arose to learn at first hand German points of view.

Broadly speaking, studying the German people was strangely like seeing ourselves in a glass; every grade of political thought and every phase of human feeling that we are familiar with here is to be found reflected there; and the thought leaps to the mind – how alike we are!

Yet one great exception there seemed to be – namely, that while the majority of English people appear to want to fight on, the majority of the Germans as clearly appear to wish for peace. From all ranks and sections I heard the same thing: 'We do not wish to continue fighting, but if we must, we can.'

I heard this most forcibly from the lips of a high official of the Foreign Office. He told me that Germany wished for peace, and was willing to enter into negotiations to that end, but he reiterated that he feared there was no such disposition on the part of English statesmen. He said he could not conceive that any country could gain anything by a continuance of the war.

He reminded me of the fact – very real to them if not understood here – that twice Germany had plainly set forth to the world that she desired peace. He said the only reply to those statements of her willingness had been insults. He felt that under these circumstances it was for our side to make the next move.

He showed that there was no idea of approaching the question of peace in Germany as victor, for he said these words: 'We know England is not beaten. It is true Germany has had great victories, but she has also had great defeats; England may not have had great victories, but neither has she suffered great defeats. We know full well that England is not defeated.'

He said that if the Allies would not speak of peace, then Germany must fight on. She could do so, because her desire for peace was not based on weakness or failing resources, but upon reason and humanity. They could fight on, if need be, for years.

He spoke freely of the food supply of Germany. Though gravely affected by our blockade, the shortage is not such as will influence the question of peace. They would be content, he affirmed, to live very plainly as in the days before 1870.

He dwelt on the horror, not solely for Germany, but for all Western Europe, of this extermination of its youth. He spoke much of the necessity for England and Germany to live in amity; race, kinship, interests all demand it.

He showed me they were prepared to be moderate and reasonable in the proposals on their side, but such intricate matters I will not approach. This and much more he said to me.

Sir, does it not seem as if negotiations might easily be opened? If the moral courage of the governments equalled the immortal military courage of their soldiers, private conversations between ministers might begin, and a basis for honorable peace be found by nobler, saner methods than those that shock the world to-day. – Yours &c, .

Emily Hobhouse
October 12th, 1916.

(This letter should be viewed in conjuncture with the correspondence with Jagow 20–24 June from the German Foreign Office files.)

The whole peace plan now became much clearer. It may be that Jagow talked as he did expecting Emily to pass the message on to her friends in England, but Emily of course saw much further. She saw it as an argument for peace and was anxious to grab any opportunity to further the peace process.

The British press took a hard line. Some expected her to be interned. Other people were kinder, for instance an acquaintance, Marguerite Bennett, wrote of her and her husband's 'great admiration for your courageous stand in the interests of truth and a more sane outlook … I understand, feeling in the country is gradually becoming more temperate, in spite of the virulent tone of the press …'

The Foreign Office deferred the situation to the Attorney General's Office, whose advisors stated that Emily had broken no laws in going to Germany, though they were aware that the Foreign Office would have liked it otherwise! The law could, however, be amended so that people could not travel to enemy countries in time of war without permission.[22]

The Foreign Office then decided it would divert the questions in the House from the disclosures in Emily's letter to the safer ground of her passport and visas, because not only had it failed to interview Miss Hobhouse but it had also failed to consider the possibility of a negotiated peace.

As could be expected, the government was successful. The first questions in the House of Commons came on 26 October, asking whether Emily had obtained permission from the Foreign Office to go to Belgium. Was Cecil aware she had gone to Germany and by whose permission?

In the ensuing days Cecil cleverly wove a web round Fortress Foreign Office. It could let in whom it liked, and see whom it liked, and it did not like to see Miss Emily Hobhouse. This was made abundantly clear. It did not approve of her seeing a high-ranking German official, it did not approve of her going to the camp for internees, and it did not approve of her going to Belgium. She may have broken no laws but in its view she had violated the passport regulations and in that she was despicable. So with the flick of a pen and a few well-chosen words Cecil all but blasted Emily to obscurity.

As a result of his last statement R.L. Outhwaite asked if the 'Hon. gentleman [had] any reason to doubt the accuracy of *The Times* report; and, if that is so, is not all this fuss about Miss Hobhouse absurd?'[23]

In the Lords a better mood prevailed, even though Lord Crewe, who took the questions, introduced a new violation – Emily had had no visa to stop in Switzerland. Some members then said they would have liked her interned. Lord Crewe was quick to point out she had not committed an indictable offence but that the law concerning visits to enemy countries would be altered.

It was Leonard Courtney who spoke up for her.[24] He said:

… but I suppose the simple fact is that, having been brooding over the state of Europe and thinking probably of the possibility of getting a stop put to the horror which is overflowing the Continent, and thinking as some of us do, that there have been grave misunderstandings on both sides which want clearing up so as to bring about the restoration of Europe to peace, she was moved – as a friend of humanity, may I say, might easily be moved, whether man or woman – on her way back from Italy to this country to go from Berne into Germany to ascertain something which might be of use, not to Germany, not to her own country above all other countries, but which might be of use to her own country and to all Europe. Now that is the action, be it wise or otherwise – a noble act of supreme tenderness, or a foolish act of self-belief. That is the action for which you must arraign her – that having gone to Italy in discharge of her intention, having deceived nobody therein she, during her winter of absence was moved to try to get into Germany as she did, and ascertain some things which she thought might be useful for the restoration of international peace. That is her offence. It is not an offence against the law …

The Midland Convention of the No-Conscription Fellowship passed a resolution on 5 November:[25]

> That this Convention desires to express its profound gratitude to Miss Emily Hobhouse for her courageous action in the cause of peace, and its sympathy with her in the hostility and misrepresentation now directed against her.

15

THE WEARY WORLD
WAITS

Both in Britain and in Germany the guard was changing. In Britain, Asquith was replaced by David Lloyd George as Premier. Lloyd George had, since the beginning of the war, lost his radical tendencies. He had been very successful as Minister for Munitions and was far more forceful than his predecessor. Like many in Britain he believed in the 'knock-out blow'. Many in his cabinet were Conservatives. The Liberals were divided or gone, and the nearly blind Viscount Grey, who had taken the country into war, resigned. Only Lord Robert Cecil remained, still as Minister for the Blockade and Undersecretary at the Foreign Office.

In Germany the formidable Ludendorff and Hindenburg now had command of the army, though the Kaiser, in theory, retained overall responsibility. Ludendorff's influence was felt everywhere, even in politics. The use and expansion of submarine warfare was now a major issue. Wilhelm II was not happy about it and, with Bethmann Hollweg, for a time managed to avert it. He told Bethmann Hollweg he was genuinely weary of the war and that to make peace 'was a moral act appropriate to a Monarch who has a soul, and feels himself responsible to God, who has a feeling for his people and the enemy's'.[1]

Germany made a formal offer of peace on 12 December 1916. It was signed by the Chancellor. Gottlieb von Jagow, who had resigned in mid-

November, possibly pushed by Ludendorff, said he helped craft it. It is a clumsy document stating all the territorial gains Germany had made and none of the concessions it might be prepared to make.[2]

This peace offer was leaked to the press in the Netherlands before reaching Allied hands so there was no way that the matter could be kept from the public. US Ambassador Gerard, felt that the terms would be impossible for the Allies to accept as they would leave Germany 'immensely powerful' and ready to take up arms again at any time.[3] Leonard Hobhouse, however, felt it was the beginning of the end. 'Though,' he added gloomily to his son: 'one could never tell with a firebrand like Lloyd George.'[4]

At about this time President Woodrow Wilson was asking the belligerents about their war aims with a view to offering mediation. This caused some consternation among the Allies who did not really want American interference. In any case they rejected the German peace initiative. Wilhelm was then reported to have grown very angry, declaring Germany must fight to the end, annex Belgium, subdue France and so on.[5]

Charles Trevelyan, a founder member of the UDC, was sending messages to America to encourage President Wilson. Wilson had come to believe the Germans were prepared for peace 'without victory' but changed his mind when the Germans announced they were going to greatly increase submarine warfare and bring it into the Atlantic.[6] Germany hoped to starve Britain out. There were great losses with food shortages and so on felt in England. However, contrary to German expectations, Britain did not fall, and in April 1917 the Americans came into the war on the Allied side.

Early in March Emily received the sad news from Isabella Steyn that her husband, the former President of the Orange Free State, had died. Emily said she greatly missed him:

As one I so truly honoured and admired ... [She was feeling much for South Africa that day] with the tidings of the loss of the transport in a channel fog with 615 poor Zulus on board ... I do so hate this bringing over of those poor fellows ... [she had heard that her friend General Smuts was on his way to London. He had been in command of the Imperial Army in Tanganyka, East Africa – formerly a German colony – and was to attend the Imperial War Conference in London] Fancy his sitting alongside Milner* ... The wheel of time brings curious changes and one hardly knows where one is.'[7]

When Jan Smuts arrived, Emily immediately implored him to work for a negotiated peace.[8]

> Victory is a Will o' the Wisp enticing both sides to their doom ... Be our help and saviour dear Oom in this grave and terrible hour. You can see more clearly than most ... Every principle of humanity calls us to stop this slaughter. War is the wrong way of settling differences – and indeed it never settles anything for long. In the end you must come together and discuss matters and use reason and goodwill; therefore do that now before greater disaster and bloodshed occurs.

Emily wanted to go to Germany herself and believed she could find out what Germany wanted and help resolve the issue. 'Let me be the bridge,' she implored: 'It need never be known ... I ask nothing better in life ...'

But Smuts, in spite of his position or because of it, would not or could not do anything. He was much in demand as a speaker and as a conciliator, and is also credited with starting the British Royal Air Force.[9] In June 1917, he was invited to join the British War Cabinet.

Thanking Smuts for a book of speeches on 12 July 1917, Emily wrote that she was glad to have it:

> ... in recollection of your English visit and shall value it as your gift ... I don't agree with all of it as you know but like the Curate's Egg** feel they are good 'in parts', and where good, very good ...
>
> As to Bethmann Hollweg if you and your government are trying to oust him I think you are making a very great and first class mistake and if you are sending emissaries to Germany to stir up internal trouble to that end it is a still greater error ... Leave them alone and they will democratise themselves. Do you want an extremist in like von Tirpitz or even von Bülow [not the same man Emily mentions below]?[10]

---

* Lord Milner had been High Commissioner when Emily first went to South Africa in the Anglo-Boer War. He had originally supported her. Smuts had worked with Milner after that war. Lloyd George, who appreciated Milner's organisational abilities, brought him into the War Cabinet as Minister without Portfolio.

** This refers to a humorous joke in the magazine *Punch* about an insecure curate breakfasting with his bishop.

She had faith in Bethmann Hollweg and again wanted to go to Germany.

Many in Germany wanted peace. Matthias Erzberger, a member of the Catholic Centre Party, proposed and carried in the Reichstag on 19 July 1917 what was called a non-binding 'Peace Resolution'. However, as it left no room for annexations Bethmann Hollweg felt unable to support it and resigned.

Erzberger believed that economics was the solution. Following the vote he went to Zurich. In the *Neue Züricher Nachrichten*, copied by *The Times*, 30 July 1917, it was reported that he said: 'If I could only have an opportunity of talking with Mr Lloyd George, or Mr Balfour [now Foreign Minister] or their trusted representative we could in a few hours reach an understanding as to a basis for peace which would enable official negotiations to begin immediately.' Erzberger said the new Chancellor's mission was peace. However, Britain still believed that the 'knock-out blow' was the only option and was not to be tempted.

In an undated letter to Smuts, which looks more like a draft and which Emily said she found in her coat pocket, she said: 'Let me talk to Herr Erzberger and then put it in official hands. So great is the need, I urge this at the risk of wearying you …'.[11]

Emily was soon pursuing another idea and on 29 August wrote to Smuts:[12] 'I want your help about something good and saving – not destroying.' She wanted parole for Baron von Bülow, who was interned in an officers' camp, although he was a civilian. She said she would supervise his parole: 'Nothing but good would come of granting him this alleviation.' She would, in fact, have liked to be allowed to organise ten-day furloughs for all internees 'suffering from mental trouble at the stage when it could be arrested!' The futility of it all irked her. She said what many others will have felt: 'the blood-stained weeks creep on – the world is weary – the winter is dreaded …'.

About this time, talks about peace were going on at a conference in Austria–Hungary. Possibly Emily knew some of the delegates from her time in Rome. In 1915 she had been in contact with the Austria-Hungarian envoys and had hoped to go to Galicia – then part of Austria-Hungarian Empire, now part of Poland and the Ukraine.

We are not sure what Emily's thought was but, probably realising that Smuts was unlikely to help, she appealed directly to Lord Milner as the leading member in the War Cabinet, to forward an offer of services to the Prime Minister.

But instead, Milner put her letter in Smuts hands and he did not support her. She was bitterly disappointed. It was Michaelmas Day 1917 (29 September)[13] and she prefaced her letter to Smuts: 'St Michael fought the dragon and prevailed' and with a quote from Psalms 55 (v.12 and 14), the psalm of the day: 'For it is not an open enemy that has done me this dishonour for then I could have borne it, but it was even thou my familiar friend whom I trusted.' It was a long letter answering him point by point: 'You do not know me – never did – therefore you cannot judge for what I am fitted …'

Although nothing was done with Emily's suggestion, later in the year Smuts was sent to try and negotiate, but it seemed Austria–Hungary was too closely tied with the fortunes of Germany for anything to come of it.[14]

On 6 January 1918, which Emily underlined as Epiphany she wrote Smuts a letter which she marked as private:[15]

> Dear Oom,
>
> You ask – is there no 'Hand Outstretched' any more? Surely there is, were there but the disposition to seize it. Take for instance the Pope – yet he was scorned and ignored. Now again he speaks and I find his Xmas speech to his Cardinals full of wise things. I begin to agree with him that (as he words it) there will be no peace till 'men turn again to God'. Avoiding religious formulas such as his and others similar to it, it is more and more impressed upon me that what must take place is the underlying change of attitude typified by that and kindred expressions.

She went on to say that nations as well as individuals needed to humble themselves, had to own error – had to confess it openly, had to admit their aims and demands were not always right, had to learn to live and let live: 'Russia, through her idealists, has pierced the heart of the matter.' She saw that: 'Peace will not come through Victory but that Victory will come through peace.' The Russia of Lenin was suing for peace, and a very harsh peace it turned out to be. Lenin later annulled this Treaty of Brest Litovsk. Emily said: 'Brush aside efforts for diplomatic triumphs, take the stand on the broad basis of truth and principle.' She raised three things that were needed to be accepted:

1. Acknowledge that guilt lies equally among all.*
2. Meet and discuss on equal terms.
3. No nation deserves to gain anything by the war.

---

* Under the Treaty of Versailles Germany was forced to accept a War Guilt clause. For many in Germany this was the most contentious issue.

If this were done, she said, 'Militarism would be defeated in its ends in all countries and a Community of equal nations would arise from the wreckage.' She said she had preached this doctrine since October 1914 – 'in season and out of season'.

For the rest of the war, Emily continued to press for a negotiated peace but one must surmise her efforts were limited. She presented some lectures in the country about a League of Nations. Her feelings were for internationalism and for the people. She was harsh on those who could not accept her view and they were harsh on her. Perhaps it was because in war people are so polarised they forget that in the past they were friends. Emily tried to show that in many cases the enemy was not as bad as suggested. In the Second World War, the Nazis could take the blame: before there was no such designation and people were afraid to blame the Prussian Junkers outright. At the end of the war there was a move to hang the Kaiser, but he was safely in Holland and the Dutch refused to deport him.

One negative trait in Emily's character was that she could exaggerate in trying to simplify a situation, as she did in giving Dr Page, the American Ambassador, the impression that she was part of a committee working for the internees, whereas she had no official position (though she did not say that she had). This was a tendency that Leonard was wary of and which the Foreign Office did not like. When, in December 1916, there was a question of a piece in an American paper which did not sound right, it questioned her through the Press Bureau and after she denied having given an interview to that paper,[16] it told the British Ambassador in Washington that he need not take her denial too seriously – which does seem rather unnecessary.

Emily knew her brother very well and no doubt hoped at Bude in the summer of 1916 that he would be turned around to support the peace initiative, but it was not to be. It was a daring plan which might have been worked out in many different ways. Leonard was much more hopeful in the case of the Kaiser's peace plan at Christmas.

In late September 1918, Ludendorff had told the Kaiser that they were in a militarily impossible situation and must have peace. At the same time, in his autocratic way, he said that the government must be reformed. A new Chancellor, Prince Max of Baden, was brought in. Prince Max at once set about asking the Americans to arrange an armistice, and also to reform the government, which he wanted to do, with the 'majority' Socialists taking a part in the running of the country for the very first time.

On 28 October the sailors in Kiel mutinied. They wanted peace and bread. Events followed quickly with the kings – rulers – of many of the twenty-eight states of the German Federation abdicating – that is except for the Kaiser. He was also King of Prussia, the biggest state, and held on for the time being.

There was revolution. The parties on the left side of the majority Socialists wanted a republic, Bolshevik-style. By 11 November, when the war ended, streams of red Bolshevik flags were flying in Berlin and other cities; the Kaiser was gone as was Prince Max, who had resigned. His job was taken on by Frederich Ebert, a democrat of the SPD – the majority Socialist Party. He was joined by Hugo Haase of the left-wing Independent Socialist Party. Because of ideological differences such a union could only be unhappy.[17]

On 11 November the Allies celebrated peace with great rejoicing. The Germans too were pleased with peace – and the reform of government – but as they contemplated those red flags, they must have wondered whether they were living in a Bolshevik state or a democratic republic – and what the future would hold.

The sequel to the present story will be told in *Living the Love,* for peace did not come quietly to the invalid Miss Hobhouse. Her sympathies were soon aroused by the plight of starving people in Europe. There was the 'Russian Babies Fund' which she started; then the Swiss railway workers who were bringing half-starved Austrian children to recuperate with Swiss families in the Alps found they were short of money and it was suggested they appeal to her, so she started a fund to help them and soon expanded this program to help German children as well. Germany and Austria were very short of food and Emily went on to provide a feeding program for 11,000 half-starved children in the industrial city of Leipzig. People in South Africa raised money to help her.

Emily Hobhouse could not save the world but she did her personal best to bring healing and reconciliation between peoples.

Notes and Sources

1 A Cornish Background

1. EH to I. Steyn, 27 April 1924
2. Young India and Natal Witness, date uncertain; 'She was one of the noblest and bravest of women … She feared no man because she feared God only.' M.K. Gandhi

2 The Beginning

1. JHB collection
2. Jagow, *England und der Kriegsausbruch* p. 3
3. Oxford and Asquith, *Memories and Reflections* vol. 2 p. 6
4. JHB collection
5. Patterson, *The Search for Negotiated Peace* pp. 30–2
6. Ibid.
7. JHB collection
8. Ibid.
9. EH Journal, 'The Story of my visit to Germany. June 7–June 24, 1916. During the Great War' pp. 1–3
10. JHB collection
11. EH to J.C. Smuts, 8 August 1914

12. JHB collection
13. TNA (British National Archives, Kew) CAB 24/34 *Pacifism*
14. JHB collection
15. Meintjes, *General Louis Botha* pp. 215–26
16. JHB collection
17. Bloemfontein Archives, Isabella Steyn Collection
18. EH to J.C. Smuts, 29 October 14
19. JHB collection
20. Meintjes p. 249
21. *Jus Suffragii*, 1 January 1915, p. 228
22. JHB collection
23. Ibid.

3 1915

1. TNA CAB24/34 *Pacifism*
2. In *Selections from the Smuts Papers* vol. III, EH/JCS, vol. 13 p. 56
3. International Congress of Women Report
4. Correspondence with Jane Addams, Swarthmore College
5. Ibid.
6. International Congress of Women Report
7. TNA FO 371/2567 no. 82596
8. Correspondence, Swarthmore College
9. Cecil, *All the Way* p. 130
10. TNA FO371/2567 no. 1243191
11. German records
12. EH Journal vol. 1 pp. 3–8
13. International Congress of Women Report
14. Ibid.
15. JHB collection
16. Ibid.
17. German records
18. Jane Addams papers, Swarthmore College
19. Patterson, p. 156
20. Ibid. p. 165; Alice Hamilton to EH, 4 December 1915, JHB collection

4 Hard Knocks

1. Kaminski, *Emily Hobhouse – The Radicalization of a Ministering Angel* (PhD thesis, University of Connecticut) p. 299, card EH to Aletta Jacobs, 26 October 1915. 'Lucy and I quite enjoyed being undressed at Tilbury. It was a new experience and as I tell her she will one day relate the adventure to her grandchildren.', Aletta Jacobs archives
2. Jane Addams papers, Swarthmore College
3. Ibid.
4. TNA FO 163590/82506 enc B, Kaminski 300
5. J.C. Smuts to EH, JHB collection
6. Aletta Jacobs correspondence, Amsterdam
7. Ibid.
8. TNA FO 163590/82506 enc. C; Kaminski p. 303
9. TNA FO187392/83506 enc. A
10. TNA FO 372/894 no.127435; Kaminski p. 303
11. EH to Aletta Jacobs, Aletta Jacobs correspondence, Amsterdam
12. Ibid., 12 February 1916
13. Oxford and Asquith, p. 143
14. Aletta Jacobs correspondence, Amsterdam
15. Noble, *War on War;* list of attendance at conference, JHB collection

5 Prelude to her Journey

1. TNA FO 372/894
2. Ibid.
3. Ibid.
4. German records
5. Ibid.
6. Kaminski p. 304
7. EH Journal vol. 1 pp. 10–12

6 Emily's Journal: Wartime Journey across Germany

1. EH Journal vol. 1 pp. 12–26

7 Emily's Journal: Into Belgium – June 1916

1. EH Journal vol. 1 p. 27–vol. 2 p. 14

8 Emily's Journal: Berlin

1. Journal vol. 2 pp. 15–85
2. GFO (German Foreign Office, acknowledgement to Akten der Politischen Abteilung des Auswärtigen Amtes, Berlin, Archivband R 20465), D937560–3)
3. Ibid., D959722–3
4. Ibid., D937564–70
5. Ibid., D959728–31 or D937571–4 – there are two separate versions of this letter
6. Ibid., D937579–81
7. Ibid., D959725–6

9 Emily's Journal: Disaster and the Return to England

1. Journal vol. 2 p. 85–vol. 3 p. 31

10 The Citadel

1. Cecil, *All the Way p.* 128
2. Taylor, *English History 1914–1945* p. 65
3. FO 372/894
4. Kaminski p. 311
5. EH to Aletta Jacobs, Aletta Jacobs correspondence, Amsterdam. The letter arrived unsigned.
6. Kaminski p. 311
7. Ibid.
8. Kaminski p. 312
9. JHB Collection
10. Ibid.
11. Kaminski p. 313

12. GFO D959717–8
13. Kaminski p. 313

11 Diary, July 1916

1. TNA FO372/894; Kaminski p. 304
2. Ibid., p. 314
3. Lord Newton diaries,
4. JHB collection
5. Ibid.
6. Kaminski p. 315; FO 372/894
7. JHB collection
8. TNA FO 372/894
9. Kaminski p. 315
10. JHB collection
11. Kaminski p. 316; FO382/1167
12. Ibid.
13. JHB collection

12 Ruhleben and Peace

1. JHB collection
2. Ibid.
3. John Hall *That Bloody Woman* p. 256
4. Kaminski p. 317
5. Ibid. p. 318; JHB collection
6. Kaminski pp. 318–19; JHB collection
7. Ibid.
8. Ibid.
9. Ibid.
10. Ibid.
11. Ibid.
12. JHB collection

13 August 1916 – Cloak and Dagger

1. JHB collection
2. Ibid., letter from German Section of the US Embassy, 5 August 1916, signature unclear
3. JHB collection
4. Ibid.
5. Ibid.
6. Ibid.
7. Ibid.
8. Ibid., 11 December 1916. Literally 'As for Stephen I've no patience with him at all ... Other people think their bodies of great value and their souls of little and are quite willing to give up the former and I don't see why if he holds the converse views, he shouldn't be willing to sacrifice his [?] soul.'
9. JHB collection
10. Ibid.
11. Ibid.
12. Ibid.
13. Ibid.
14. Ibid.
15. GFO D959720
16. From German files, verbal information
17. Ibid.
18. JHB collection
19. Hansard 15 November 1916

14 Belgium, Peace and the Push Back

1. Archives Bloemfontein
2. JHB collection
3. K.E. Markel to EH, 29 August 1916, JHB collection
4. W.A.M. Goode to EH, 18 August 1916
5. October 1916, *Woman's Dreadnought* p. 567
6. Strumm to Romberg, GFO files, Berne
7. JHB collection
8. *The Herald*, 21 October 1916
9. Zuckerman, *The Rape of Belgium* p. 274

10. JHB collection
11. Newton, *Retrospection* p. 261
12. JHB collection
13. Swartz, *The Union of Democratic Control* p. 170
14. *The Times*, 18–21 October 1916
15. Ibid.
16. TNA FO372/894
17. Gooch, *Life of Lord Courtney* p. 660
18. Archbishop of Canterbury to EH 10 October 1916, JHB collection
19. EH to Archbishop of Canterbury, 13 October 1916, JHB collection
20. GFO files, pencilled remark
21. German Berne files
22. TNA FO371
23. Hansard, House of Commons debate, 1 November 1916 1698
24. Hansard, House of Lords debate, 1 November 1916 377–8
25. JHB collection

15 The Weary World Waits

1. Clark *Kaiser Wilhelm II* p. 324
2. TNA CAB 23 1
3. Gerard, *My Four Years in Germany*
4. Leonard Hobhouse to EH, JHB collection
5. Clark, p. 324
6. Patterson, pp. 277, 298, 301
7. Bloemfontein Archives
8. EH to J.C. Smuts, 25 March 1917, no. 195
9. Hancock, *Smuts, 1: The Sanguine Years* p. 438
10. EH to J.C. Smuts, vol. 16 no. 218
11. Ibid., undated vol. 16 no. 221
12. Ibid., No. 224
13. Ibid., No. 226A
14. Taylor p. 158
15. EH to J.C. Smuts, vol. 20, no. 11
16. Kaminski, p. 335
17. Ryder *The German Revolution*, 154

BIBLIOGRAPHY

Andrew, Christopher, *Secret Service: The Making of the British Intelligence Community* (London: Heinemann, 1985)

Balme, Jennifer Hobhouse, *To Love One's Enemies* (Cobble Hill, British Columbia: Hobhouse Trust, 1994)

Baranowski, Shelley, *The Sanctity of Rural Life: Nobility, Protestantism, and Nazism in Weimar Prussia* (New York and London: Oxford University Press, 1995)

Beaverbrook, Lord, *The Decline and Fall of Lloyd George* (London: Collins, 1963)

Bessel, Richard, *Germany After the First World War* (Oxford: Clarendon Press, 1993)

Brockway, Fenner, *Socialism over Sixty Years: The Life of Jowett of Bradford* (London: George Allen and Unwin, 1946)

Bussey, Gertrude and Tims, Margaret, *Pioneers for Peace: Women's International League for Peace and Freedom 1915–1965* (London: WILPF British Section, 1980)

Cecil, Lord Robert, (Viscount Cecil of Chelwood), *All the Way* (London: Hodder & Stoughton, 1949)

Clark, Christopher, *Kaiser Wilhelm II* (London: Penguin, 2009)

Clayton, Joseph, *The Rise and Decline of Socialism in Great Britain 1884–1924* (London: Faber & Gwyer, 1926)

David, Edward, ed., *Inside Asquith's Cabinet, From the Diaries of Charles Hobhouse* (London: John Murray, 1977)

Dowse, Robert E., *Left in the Centre: The Independent Labour Party* (London: Longmans, 1966)

Elton, Lord Godfrey, *The Life of James Ramsay MacDonald (1866–1919)* (London: Collins, 1939)

Fischer, Louis, *The Life of Lenin* (New York, Evanston and London: Harper and Row, 1964)

Gerard, James W. *My Four Years in Germany* (New York: George H. Doran Company, 1917)

Gooch, G.P., *Life of Lord Courtney* (1920)

Grew, Joseph C., *Turbulent Era – A Diplomatic Record of Forty Years 1904–1945 vol. 1* (Boston: Houghton Mifflin Co., 1963)

Halperin, S. William, *Germany Tried Democracy – A Political History of the Reich from 1918–1933* (New York: The Norton Library, 1946)

Hanan, June and Hunt, Karen *Socialist Women: Britain, 1880s to 1920s* (London and New York: Routledge, 2002)

Hancock, W.K., *Smuts, 1: The Sanguine Years 1870–1919* (Cambridge University Press, 1962)

Hancock, W.K., *Selections from the Smuts Papers Volume III and IV 1910–1919* (Cambridge University Press, 1966)

Hobhouse, Emily, *Boer War Letters,* ed. Rykie van Reenen (Cape Town: Human & Rousseau, 1984)

Hobhouse, Emily, *The Brunt of the War and Where it Fell* (London: Methuen, 1903)

Hobhouse, L.T., *The World in Conflict* (London: T. Fisher Unwin, 1915)

Hobhouse, L.T., *Questions of War and Peace* (London: T. Fisher Unwin, 1916)

Hobhouse, L.T. and Hammond, J.L., *Memoir of Lord Hobhouse* (London, Edward Arnold, 1905)

Horne, John and Kramer, Alan, *German Atrocities, 1914: A History of Denial* (New Haven: Yale University Press, 2001)

Jagow, Gottlieb von, *England und der Kriegsausbruch* (Berlin: 1925)

Jones, Mary Hoxie *Swords into Ploughshares – An Account of the American Friends Service Committee 1917–1937* (New York: The Macmillan Company, 1937)

Leitner, Gerit von, *Wollen wir unsere Hände in Unschuld waschen? Gertrud Woker 1878–1968* (Berlin: Weidler Buchverlag, 1998)

Link, Arthur S., *Woodrow Wilson: A Brief Biography* (Cleveland, New York: World Publishing Co., 1963)

Meintjes, Johannes, *General Louis Botha* (London: Cassell, 1979)

Moorhead, Caroline, *Troublesome People: The Warriors of Pacifism* (Bethesda, USA: Adler & Adler, 1983)

Nation, R. Craig, *War on War* (Chicago: Haymarket Books, 2009; first published Durham NC: Duke University Press, 1989)

Newton, Lord, *Retrospection* (London: 1941)

Owen, Frank, *Tempestuous Journey: Lloyd George, His Life and Times* (London: Hutchinson, 1954)

Oxford, Earl of and Asquith, K.G., *Memories and Reflections* vol. 2 (London: Cassell and Co, 1928)

Patterson, David S., The Search for Negotiated Peace: Women's Activism and Citizen Diplomacy in World War I (London: Routledge, 2004)

Ryder, A.J., *The German Revolution of 1918: A Study of German Socialism in War and Revolt* (Cambridge University Press, 1967)

Seibold, Birgit Susanne, *Emily Hobhouse and the Reports on the Concentration Camps during the Boer War 1899–1902* (Stuttgart: Ibidem, 2011)

Swartz, Marvin J., *The Union of Democratic Control in British Politics during the First World War* (Oxford: Oxford University Press, 1971)

Taylor, A.J.P., *English History 1914–1945* (New York and London: Oxford University Press, 1965)

Watt, Richard M., *The King's Depart: The Tragedy of Germany, Versailles and the German Revolution* (New York: Simon and Schuster, 1968)

Wilson, Trevor, *The Downfall of the Liberal Party 1914–1935* (Ithica, New York: Cornell University Press, 1966)

Zuckerman, Larry, *The Rape of Belgium: The Untold Story of World War 1* (New York: New York University Press, 2004)

INDEX

If you enjoyed this book, you may also be interested in...

Great War Britain: The First World War at Home
LUCINDA GOSLING

The declaration of war in 1914 was to change Britain irrevocably as conflict came to dominate almost every aspect of civilian life. Popular magazines such as *The Tatler*, *The Sketch* and *The Queen* recorded the preoccupations of the time Targeted at a well-heeled, largely female audience, these magazines were veteran reporters of fashion, balls and society engagements, but quickly adapted to war conditions without ever quite losing their gossipy essence. Fashion and Court presentations soon found themselves jostling for position with items on patriotic fundraising and nursing convalescent soldiers. The result is a fascinating, at times amusing and uniquely feminine and upper-class perspective of life on the home front during the First World War.

978 0 7524 9188 2

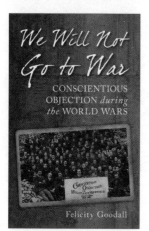

We Will Not Go To War: Conscientious Objection during the World Wars
FELICITY GOODALL

During the First and Second World Wars thousands of men and women refused the call to arms. Reviled, starved and beaten, theirs was a battle of conscience. In the First World War, seventy-three conscientious objectors died as a result of their treatment, and hundreds more were imprisoned, while others performed other, non-combatant duties with great heroism Unable to turn a blind eye to the dark realities of war, these men and women, who came from all classes and backgrounds, wrestled with their moral values, and their struggles, motivations and stories are brought together in this moving and challenging history of war's outcasts.

978 0 7524 5857 1

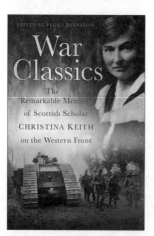

War Classics: The Remarkable Memoir of Scottish Scholar Christina Keith on the Western Front
FLORA JOHNSTON

Christina Keith came from the small town of Thurso on the far north coast of Scotland. Highly intelligent and ambitious, she became a lecturer in Classics at a time when that was still a brave and unusual choice for a woman. Towards the end of the First World War she left behind the sheltered world of academia to live and work among soldiers of all social backgrounds as a lecturer with the Army's education scheme in France. She writes with warmth and humour of her experiences. When she and a companion travel across the devastated battlefi elds, just a short time after the guns have fallen silent, her descriptions are both evocative and moving. This unique memoir is an unforgettable read.

978 0 7509 5366 5

Visit our website and discover thousands of other History Press books.

www.thehistorypress.co.uk